GOD'S LOVERS IN AN AGE OF ANXIETY

TRADITIONS OF CHRISTIAN SPIRITUALITY SERIES

GOD'S LOVERS IN AN AGE OF ANXIETY

The Medieval English Mystics

JOAN M. NUTH

SERIES EDITOR:
Philip Sheldrake

DARTON · LONGMAN + TODD

First published in 2001 by
Darton, Longman and Todd Ltd
1 Spencer Court
140–142 Wandsworth High Street
London SW18 4JJ

ISBN 0–232–52335–5

A catalogue record for this book is available from the British Library.

Phototypeset in 10/13¼pt New Century Schoolbook
by Intype London Ltd
Printed and bound in Great Britain by
The Bath Press, Bath

HOLLOWAY

CONTENTS

CONTENTS

PREFACE TO THE SERIES

Nowadays, in the Western world, there is a widespread hunger for spirituality in all its forms. This is not confined to traditional religious people let alone to regular churchgoers. The desire for resources to sustain the spiritual quest has led many people to seek wisdom in unfamiliar places. Some have turned to cultures other than their own. The fascination with Native American or Aboriginal Australian spiritualities is a case in point. Other people have been attracted by the religions of India and Tibet or the Jewish Kabbalah and Sufi mysticism. One problem is that, in comparison to other religions, Christianity is not always associated in people's minds with 'spirituality'. The exceptions are a few figures from the past who have achieved almost cult status such as Hildegard of Bingen or Meister Eckhart. This is a great pity, for Christianity East and West over two thousand years has given birth to an immense range of spiritual wisdom. Many traditions continue to be active today. Others that were forgotten are being rediscovered and reinterpreted.

It is a long time since an extended series of introductions to Christian spiritual traditions has been available in English. Given the present climate, it is an opportune moment for a new series which will help more people to be aware of the great spiritual riches available within the Christian tradition.

The overall purpose of the series is to make selected spiritual traditions available to a contemporary readership. The books seek to provide accurate and balanced historical and thematic treatments of their subjects. The authors are also conscious of the need to make connections with contemporary experience and values without being artificial or reducing a tradition to one dimension. The authors are well versed in reliable scholarship about the traditions they describe. However, their intention is that the books should be fresh in style and accessible to the general reader.

One problem that such a series inevitably faces is the word 'spirituality'. For example, it is increasingly used beyond religious circles and does not necessarily imply a faith tradition. Again, it could mean substantially different things for a Christian and a Buddhist. Within Christianity itself, the word in its modern sense is relatively recent. The reality that it stands for differs subtly in the different contexts of time and place. Historically, 'spirituality' covers a breadth of human experience and a wide range of values and practices.

No single definition of 'spirituality' has been imposed on the authors in this series. Yet, despite the breadth of the series there is a sense of a common core in the writers themselves and in the traditions they describe. All Christian spiritual traditions have their source in three things. First, while drawing on ordinary experience and even religious insights from elsewhere, Christian spiritualities are rooted in the Scriptures and particularly in the Gospels. Second, spiritual traditions are not derived from abstract theory but from attempts to live out gospel values in a positive yet critical way within specific historical and cultural contexts. Third, the experiences and insights of individuals and groups are not isolated but are related to the wider Christian tradition of beliefs, practices and community life. From a Christian perspective, spirituality is not just concerned with prayer or even with narrowly religious activities. It concerns the whole of human life, viewed in terms of a conscious relationship with God, in Jesus Christ, through the indwelling of the Holy Spirit and within a community of believers.

The series as a whole includes traditions that probably would not have appeared twenty years ago. The authors themselves have been encouraged to challenge, where appropriate, inaccurate assumptions about their particular tradition. While conscious of their own biases, authors have none the less sought to correct the imbalances of the past. Previous understandings of what is mainstream or 'orthodox' sometimes need to be questioned. People or practices that became marginal demand to be re-examined. Studies of spirituality in the past frequently underestimated or ignored the role of women. Sometimes the treatments of spiritual traditions were culturally one-sided because they were written from an uncritical Western European or North Atlantic perspective.

However, any series is necessarily selective. It cannot hope to do full justice to the extraordinary variety of Christian spiritual traditions. The principles of selection are inevitably open to question. I hope that an appropriate balance has been maintained between a sense of the likely readership on the one hand and the dangers of narrowness on the other. In the end, choices had to be made and the result is inevitably weighted in favour of traditions that have achieved 'classic' status or which seem to capture the contemporary imagination. Within these limits, I trust that the series will offer a reasonably balanced account of what the Christian spiritual tradition has to offer.

As editor of the series I would like to thank all the authors who agreed to contribute and for the stimulating conversations and correspondence that sometimes resulted. I am especially grateful for the high quality of their work which made my task so much easier. Editing such a series is a complex undertaking. I have worked closely throughout with the editorial team of Darton, Longman and Todd and Robert Ellsberg of Orbis Books. I am immensely grateful to them for their friendly support and judicious advice. Without them this series would never have come together.

PHILIP SHELDRAKE
Sarum College, Salisbury

AUTHOR'S PREFACE

My acquaintance with the medieval English mystics began over thirty years ago, when my reading of David Knowles' *The English Mystical Tradition* whetted my appetite for serious scholarship in what was then called mystical theology. Since that time, I have studied and taught Julian's *Showings* in some depth, and Margery's *Book* to a lesser extent. I am very grateful to Philip Sheldrake for asking me to write this volume, since it enabled me to round out and deepen my appreciation for this extraordinary group of writers, and to introduce them to others. Thanks are due to him as well for his good cheer, assistance, and encouragement during the progress of this work, despite mailing and e-mailing difficulties. I thank the staff of Darton, Longman and Todd for their precise and efficient editing, excellent in every respect. Thanks also go to the administration of John Carroll University for providing course reductions which yielded the time necessary to work on this project, and to my graduate assistants, Wendy Wilkinson and Maria Karita Ivancic, SND, who performed many unglamorous research tasks needed for its completion.

Special thanks are due to the following for permission to quote copyrighted material: to Paulist Press, 997 Macarthur Blvd., Mahwah, NJ 07430, for *Richard Rolle: The English Writings*, edited by Rosamund S. Allen (1988), for *The Cloud of Unknowing*, edited by James Walsh (1981), for Walter Hilton, *The Scale of Perfection*, edited by John P.H. Clark and Rosemary Dorward (1991), for Julian of Norwich, *Showings*, edited by Edmund Colledge and James Walsh, and to Cambridge University Press, 40 West 20th Street, New York, NY 10011, for

Nicholas Watson, *Richard Rolle and the Invention of Authority*, Cambridge Studies in Medieval Literature 13 (1991).

Finally, I add a word of thanks to those who provide encouragement to me on a regular basis: to Brian McDermott, SJ who admonishes me to 'write more,' to Christine Schenk, CSJ who appreciates my theological endeavours, to my friends in the Circle of Hope who accompany me on my faith journey, to my students who challenge me, and to my colleagues in the Religious Studies Department at John Carroll who are an unending source of convivial companionship.

1. THE HISTORICAL FRAMEWORK

The history of mysticism in the Church is the history of the reaction of many different temperaments to one Reality . . . It does not put before us one particular kind of experience or one uniform type of perfection . . . Something of the natural disposition [of the mystic] will often remain, and must be taken into account by us. These human inequalities affect the self-expression of the mystic, and help to produce that variety of type which makes Christian history so rich and so interesting . . . In reading the mystics . . . we must be careful not to cut them out of their backgrounds and try to judge them by spiritual standards alone. They are human beings immersed in the stream of human history; children of their own time, their own Church, as well as children of Eternal Love. Like other human beings, that is to say, they have their social and their individual aspects; and we shall not obtain a true idea of them unless both be kept in mind.

Evelyn Underhill, *The Mystics of the Church*[1]

Fourteenth-century England produced an extraordinary flowering of religious writers. Richard Rolle, the most prolific, lived from c. 1300 to 1349. Three others flourished toward the end of the century: the anonymous author of *The Cloud of Unknowing* (fl. 1380s), Walter Hilton (d. 1395/6), and Julian of Norwich (1342–c. 1416). The pious laywoman Margery Kempe (1373–c. 1440) dictated the record of her spiritual experiences in the early fifteenth century. This book studies the spiritual legacy of this group of authors. In contrast to the other

volumes in this series, their collected works do not form a cohesive 'tradition' in the usual sense of the word, since each is
distinctively different from the others. These writers do,
however, have three things in common: all were influenced by a
common tradition of English spirituality, all wrote in English,
and all were products of the fourteenth century. These three
facts provide a framework within which to consider the insights
into spirituality of these 'medieval English mystics'.

Mysticism is a term which deserves explanation, since it can
have different shades of meaning. In Roman Catholic circles
since the Second Vatican Council, the study of mysticism has
undergone rather dramatic changes in contrast to the scholarship of the first half of the twentieth century. Scholars are
generally no longer interested in distinguishing mystical
experience so absolutely from the experience of grace shared by
all Christians, or from theology, whose object is the trinitarian
God.[2]

The theology of the German Jesuit Karl Rahner is particularly helpful for understanding the continuity between the
'ordinary' Christian life of grace and mystical experience. For
him, grace is the active presence of God in the world, affecting
and transforming all human reality. Everything good one does
happens in co-operation with and under the influence of this
divine presence. So constant and pervasive is this influence, so
united with natural human thoughts and actions, that it is
usually not noticed as something out of the ordinary. However,
on occasion, a particular experience may point to the presence
of God with unusual clarity and force. This kind of experience
always comes as a surprise, and the recipient has no doubt that
it had its source in God's gracious influence.[3]

Mystical experience is a particularly strong manifestation of
this special experience of grace, thus it is in continuity with the
'normal' Christian life of grace. There is a sense in which all
baptized Christians living a graced life are mystics, although
we usually reserve the term to describe one more acutely conscious than most of the activity of God in one's life. Mystical
experience involves an intense awareness of God's presence,

accompanied by a knowledge and love of God that are recognized as extraordinary. Such awareness is difficult to put into words, and often results in a dramatic transformation in the one who receives it.[4] Like every experience of grace, mystical experience is attributed to the utterly gratuitous love of God. It is not the result of any purely human activity, although it can be desired, petitioned, and even prepared for to some degree. However, again like every experience of grace, the action of God is mediated through the person's natural capacity to receive and understand the gift of God. God's action on the soul is always, even in the most ineffable mystical experience, a mediated immediacy. The mystic's own imagination, will and intellect are very much involved in the experience,[5] and, since these are affected by the culture in which one lives, it is important to take cultural influences into account in any description of mystical experience. Sometimes mystical experience is accompanied by certain psycho-physical phenomena, such as visions, voices, ecstasy, levitations. But these have always been regarded as secondary in importance to the actual experience of union with God. We can conclude, then, that mystics are people with a heightened consciousness of the presence of God in their lives, a consciousness which allows the power of God's grace to work in them to an extraordinary degree.

The project of this book is neither to make absolute distinctions between mystical writing and other forms of religious writing, nor to judge the degree of mystical experience enjoyed by the authors studied. Rather it intends to present their contributions to the Christian mystical tradition, hoping to encourage further reading in their texts, and hoping also that some of their insights might continue to have the power to nourish Christian life and prayer today.

THE ENGLISH SPIRITUAL TRADITION

The English mystics considered in this volume need to be placed within the context of the earlier English spiritual tradition, which itself is rooted in the broader spirituality of the continent. The most obvious continental influences on English spirituality are the Augustinian tradition, especially as developed by Hugh and Richard of St Victor,[6] and the Benedictine tradition, notably that of the twelfth-century Cistercians, headed by Bernard of Clairvaux.[7] Less strong is the influence of Franciscan[8] and Dominican spirituality.[9] In addition, Julian and Margery have affinities with continental women visionaries.[10] Continental influences were modified by native forces, producing a brand of spirituality that can be described as typically English, with the following characteristics.

First, medieval English spirituality had a deep appreciation for Scripture and the monastic tradition of *lectio divina* as foundational for growth in the life of prayer.[11] This method of Scripture interpretation includes four steps. First is the *lectio*, the reading of a scriptural passage, which was done aloud, allowing the words to be heard as well as seen, and felt by the moving of the lips. The next step is *meditatio*, through which scriptural passages were learned 'by heart'. The term 'rumination' aptly describes this step: the words of Scripture were 'chewed over' and 'digested', becoming part of one's consciousness. Meditation also involved the use of the imagination, wherein the scenes of Scripture were visualized in vivid detail, allowing one to participate in the action and feeling of the scriptural narrative. A typical meditation (on Luke 7:36–50) is found in Aelred of Rievaulx's *Rule of Life for a Recluse*:

> Now go into the Pharisee's house and see our Lord in his place at table there. Together with that most blessed sinner approach his feet, wash them with your tears, wipe them with your hair, soothe them with kisses and warm them with ointments. Are you not already penetrated with the fragrance of that sacred oil? If he still will not let you approach his feet, be insistent, beseech him, raise your eyes to him brimming with tears and extort from him with deep sighs and unutterable groanings what you seek.[12]

The third step is *oratio* (prayer), whereby the fruits of the *lectio* and *meditatio* issue into praise and/or supplication of God. In the meditation above, the anchoress is advised to beseech Jesus to let her approach him: 'How long will you turn your face away from me? How long shall I have to cry out without your listening to me? Give back to me, good Jesus, the joy of your salvation, for my heart has said to you: "I have sought your face, your face, Lord, I will seek." '[13] Finally, the goal of the whole process is *contemplatio* in which one rests silently in the presence of God, relishing the gifts of such union.

A second aspect of medieval English spirituality is its grounding in the tradition of affective piety, with its tender devotion to the humanity of Christ.[14] Anselm of Canterbury (1033–1109) is credited with the origin of this tradition towards the end of the eleventh century. His *Cur Deus homo* placed new emphasis upon the humanity and especially the death of Christ, and his *Prayers and Meditations* gave devotional expression to such emphasis through their outpourings of grief over the sufferings endured by Christ in his passion. Note, for example, the emotion expressed in the following:

> Why, O my soul, were you not there to be pierced by a
> sword of bitter sorrow when you could not bear the
> piercing of the side of your Saviour with a lance?
> Why could you not bear to see the nails violate the hands
> and feet of your Creator?
> Why did you not see with horror the blood that poured
> out of the side of your Redeemer?
> Why were you not drunk with bitter tears when they
> gave him bitter gall to drink?[15]

This new feeling toward the humanity and suffering of Christ, linked to a similar devotion to the Mother of God, spread throughout the twelfth century, led by Bernard of Clairvaux and the Cistercians, finding expression in countless meditations, poems, hymns and prayers, all designed to inspire and give voice to an intense, intimate love for the Saviour. The Franciscans brought such devotion out of the monastery into the market-place through their sermons and their advocacy of popular devotions to the infancy and passion of Christ. By the fourteenth century the influence of this movement was everywhere present.[16]

A notable flowering of this devotion is found in the medieval English lyrics, such as this example from the fourteenth century:[17]

> Jesu, swete is the love of thee,
> Noon othir thing so swete may be;
> No thing that men may heere and see
> Hath no swetnesse ayens thee . . .
>
> Jesu, thi love was us so fre
> That it fro hevene broughte thee;
> For love thou dere boughtist me,
> For love thou hynge on roode tre . . .
>
> Jesu, for love thou bood so wo
> That blody stremys runne the fro;
> Thi whyte sydes woxen blw and blo –
> Oure synnes it maden, so wolawo!
>
> Jesu, for love thou steigh on roode,
> For love thou yaf thin herte blode;
> Love thee made my soules foode,
> Thi love us bought til al goode . . .
>
> Jesu my God, Jesu my kyng,
> Thou axist me oon othir thing,
> But trewe love and herte yernyng,
> And love-teeris with swete mornyng . . . [18]

These verses illustrate major themes of the English passion lyrics: an intense, intimate relationship to Christ, deep emotionality tempered by a reflective framework, vivid details of the passion, and the fact that Christ's suffering signifies his personal love for each individual, demanding a reciprocal response.

A third characteristic of medieval English spirituality is its preference for the solitary life. There have always been hermits and anchorites in Christian history, but in England the eremitic life seems to have been more popular and more idiosyncratic than elsewhere, exhibiting what Benedicta Ward calls the 'do-it-yourself approach to solitude'.[19] Hermits lived alone in isolated places, sustaining themselves by begging or growing their own food, and performing useful work like repairing roads or bridges. Anchorites commonly lived in the towns, usually in a small cell attached to a church, and their enclosure was more permanent and strictly regulated. Unlike the practice of eremiticism on the continent, English solitaries often had no links to established religious orders or specific monasteries. Officially the eremitic life was recognized as distinct from lay, clerical and monastic life.

Medieval spiritual writings generally emphasize various degrees of perfection achievable by the Christian. Every area of medieval life was hierarchically arranged, and religious life was no exception. Thus, the monastic or cenobitic life, understood as a life devoted to contemplation, was thought to be of greater value than the active religious life of the parish priest, whose chief concern was the care of souls. Both of these were preferable to the life of the married layperson. Generally, these ways of life were considered to be mutually exclusive; it was not expected that a busy pastor, for example, would be given to contemplation. None the less, there were also attempts to describe something called the 'mixed life' combining contemplation and action. In the context of this hierarchical ordering, the solitary life was usually considered superior to the contemplative life lived in community and, indeed, the holiest form of religious life possible.[20]

The popularity of the solitary life in England gave rise to a significant body of literature written to aid its practitioners, particularly anchoresses. The Latin forerunner of the English works, *De institutione inclusarum (Rule of Life for a Recluse)*, was written around 1160 by the Yorkshire Cistercian Aelred of Rievaulx (*c.* 1110–67) ostensibly for his sister, but certainly with a wider readership in mind. Only one-third of the text recommends any external regulations. The bulk of the *Rule* is concerned with the interior life: with the dispositions requisite for solitude (chastity, custody of the senses, discretion, modesty, courage, simplicity, charity, devotion to contemplation), all with a strong focus on the love of God. It aims to inspire the single-hearted devotion of the anchoress's whole life to God: 'Put all your trust in him who feeds the birds and clothes the lilies. Let him be your barn, your storecupboard, your purse, your wealth, your delight; let him alone be all things in all.'[21]

Aelred's *Rule* provided the model for the most important religious text in English of the thirteenth century, the *Ancrene Wisse* (*Guide for Anchoresses*). Only the first and last chapters are concerned with an 'outer rule' containing guidelines for the daily life of the anchoress, which are left flexible to allow for individual circumstances. Enclosed within is the 'inner rule' in six sections, each of which treats a topic important for the spiritual welfare of the anchoress: the custody of the senses, the heart and its dispositions, temptations, confession, penance, and love as the goal of the anchoritic life. Other English works found in the same manuscripts with *Ancrene Wisse* include *Holy Maidenhood,* a letter in praise of virginity; *Sawles Warde* (*Care of the Soul*), an allegory on the importance of guarding one's soul by meditating on eternal reward or punishment; three accounts of the early martyrs: *St. Katherine, St. Margaret,* and *St. Juliana*; and several short meditations in the style of Anselm, the longest of which is *The Wooing of Our Lord.*[22] Taken together, they help us understand the motives for becoming an anchoress.

First, the life was penitential and ascetic: the anchorhold provides security against worldly danger, the devil's wiles, God's wrath, and especially the anchoress's own frailty. A strong emphasis is placed upon the need to be watchful to avoid the traps of sin. Like a bird who must occasionally descend to earth in search of food, the anchoress, when dealing with the outer world, 'must look carefully about her as a bird does, keep watch on every side, so that she does no kind of wrong – lest she be caught by some of the devil's snares, or hurt in some way, during the time she stays so low.'[23]

A second more positive motivation for the anchoritic life was its status as a life of heroism and holiness. Anchoresses are to consider themselves the spiritual descendants of the desert fathers, heroically engaged in battle with evil, enduring a kind of martyrdom. The martyrdom stories of SS Katherine, Margaret and Juliana provide female role models of heroic sanctity. One word summarizes best the goal of the anchoress's struggle against evil: purity. On the one hand, the goal was absolute purity of heart, exemplified in the willingness to endure shame and misunderstanding with humility, patience, and holy indifference, in imitation of Christ who endured his passion without complaint. On the other hand, the goal was physical purity (chastity), exemplified in the struggle against the desires of the flesh. Bodily virginity and/or the anchorhold are symbolized by a high tower that both exalts and protects. Modern commentators are shocked by the exaltation of virginity and the vilification of marriage found in the anchoritic literature, particularly in *Holy Maidenhood*,[24] which has been described as one of the 'most extreme of all the anti-sexual and anti-marital polemics in Christianity.'[25]

A third motivation for the anchoritic life, linked to the regard for virginity, is the idea that the anchoress is literally a bride of Christ. The anchorhold is not only a protecting tower, but a wedding chamber wherein the anchoress experiences union with Christ her spouse. This theme has its origins in twelfth- and thirteenth-century bridal mysticism, particularly Bernard's influential *Sermons on the Song of Songs*.[26] While Bernard presented the marriage theme as a metaphor to describe the soul's union with God, the English writers of anchoritic literature interpret it more literally. In *The Wooing of Our Lord,* for example, Christ is seen to be superior with respect to anything desirable in a prospective earthly husband: beauty, possessions, generosity, wisdom, bravery, gentleness, good family connections, and high birth. In meditating on this last, the anchoress is encouraged to pray:

> Where can I choose a nobler man than you, who are the son
> of the King who rules this world, and King and equal with
> your Father, King over kings, Lord over lords? And again,
> with respect to your manhood, you were born of Mary – a
> maiden most humble of spirit – a royal child from birth, the
> kin of king David, of Abraham's line. There is no higher
> birth than this under the sun. I will love you, then, sweet
> Jesus, as the noblest creature who ever lived on earth.[27]

I have emphasized the solitary life not only because it is
well represented in the religious literature the English mystics
would have known, but also because all of them had some
connection to it. Richard Rolle lived as a hermit for the whole of
his adult life, and extolled eremiticism in his writings. He
wrote his *Form of Living* and, almost certainly, his English
psalter commentary for Margaret Kirkeby, an anchoress. It is
likely that the author of *The Cloud* was a Carthusian, an order
of recluses, as was the young man to whom the book is
addressed. Walter Hilton lived briefly as a hermit, and Book 1
of his *Scale of Perfection* is addressed to an anchoress. Julian
was enclosed as an anchoress some time after her visionary
experience of 1373. Even Margery valued the spiritual prowess
connected with the solitary life, since she chose an anchorite for
her confessor and consulted Julian for spiritual advice.

Several other characteristics typify English spirituality:
harmony and balance between the affective and the speculative, loyalty to the institutional Church, concern for
orthodoxy, moderation in ascetical practices, and a preference
for the concrete over the abstract. This last, coupled with a
practical pastoral emphasis, is one of the most distinctive traits
of the English spiritual tradition. In summing up the anchoritic
tradition, Savage and Watson write, 'Perhaps above all else it
seems *pragmatic* in its approach to spiritual reality . . . Like all
good pastoral writings, the anchoritic works deal in their
several ways with the real world of their readers, not with
abstract theological issues and occasional spiritual possibilities.'[28] It is this characteristic, the concreteness and

practicality of English religious writing, that may have contributed to the English mystics' reputation of being 'anti-intellectual', a charge that is certainly without merit. Both Rolle and Hilton had a university education, and their writings reveal a high degree of learning, as do those of *The Cloud* author. While a formal university education was not accessible to Julian, her writing exhibits a sophisticated understanding and a unique development of doctrinal theology. Even the illiterate Margery Kempe valued learning highly, for she sought public preachers to satisfy her thirst for religious knowledge.

WRITING IN THE VERNACULAR

Around the year 1200 a significant change begins to be noticeable in Western religious literature, for these writings were at the forefront of the developing vernacular languages all over Europe. With this change, there is the appearance of other differences in the tradition. Most significant is the fact that women's voices begin increasingly to be heard. The lack of access to a classical education had prevented most women before this time, with a few notable exceptions, from expressing themselves in the Latin of ecclesial and academic discourse. Furthermore, the audience for these writings gradually expanded to embrace all those without a reading knowledge of Latin, which again included many women.

Vernacular writing, even when dependent on Latin sources, was never a case of mere translation. Because of the nature of language to give shape to thought, vernacular expression of ideas created new theological and linguistic possibilities.[29] So significant is the change associated with this movement to the vernacular, that the historian Bernard McGinn has suggested the need to recognize a third type of theology, called 'vernacular theology', to complement the scholastic and monastic theologies of the Middle Ages.[30] This vernacular theology shared with all theology the goals of encouraging greater love of God and others, and of fostering a deeper understanding of the faith. However, the way these goals were configured differed. Scholasticism gave priority to academic concerns, writing in a formal, objective style. To realize its purpose of nourishing the spiritual development of monks, monastic theology developed specific genres: the biblical commentary, treatises on various topics often in the form of letters, and highly rhetorical sermons and meditations. As this tradition developed in the twelfth and thirteenth centuries, it became more subjective, more poetic and image-filled than the language of scholasticism. Vernacular theology continued to develop some of the genres of monastic theology, such as sermons, letters, and treatises, adapting them to the needs of an audience no longer restricted to the monastic community. Hagiography, the recording of saints' lives, focusing upon the personal experience of its subjects, became a popular genre, and poetry grew in importance. Of particular significance is the genre of the visionary account, the subjects or authors of which were predominantly women.

The anchoritic works described above are the best thirteenth-century examples of England's participation in this general movement towards vernacular religious writing. Bella Millet provides a lucid account of this development, and what follows here is a summary of her thesis.[31] In the early Middle Ages, Latin was the standard written language throughout Europe, and vernacular writing was rare before 1200. To be considered literate meant that one could read and write Latin, and, except for some of the aristocracy, such literacy was limited to those in religious life. Thus those who were literate were generally called *clerici* (clerics) and those who were illiterate *laici* (laity). But everywhere people spoke in the vernacular, though the oral traditions formed through such speaking are largely lost to us. The majority of people were formed by this oral culture; therefore we ought not consider written Latin culture as solely representative of medieval societies as a whole. Millet draws a distinction between the oral tradition (consisting of poetry, songs, drama, narrative, sermons, and the like) which was composed for listening, and the classical Latin tradition, preserved in the writings handed down to us. With the shift to the vernacular, some of the spirit, style and content of this vernacular oral tradition begins to be put into writing.

Most women in England throughout the Middle Ages had no possibility of becoming literate in Latin in the full sense of the word. However, this does not mean that some of them, such as nuns who recited the Latin divine office, or educated members of the aristocracy, knew no Latin at all. The *Ancrene Wisse* expects that its readers will be familiar with the Latin psalms and other prayers, since these are found in Latin without translation within the text. However, the anchoritic life was not restricted to ex-nuns, and laywomen, such as those for whom *Ancrene Wisse* was written, also embraced this form of life, many of whom were literate in English. Millett summarizes her thesis thus:

> The lay anchoresses of the twelfth and thirteenth century seem to have been significant for the development of vernacular literature mainly because of their intermediate position between *laici* and *clerici*, illiterates and *literati*. Since reading was one of the occupations expected of a recluse, there was an incentive for their spiritual directors to supply them with (as *Ancrene Wisse* puts it) 'reading in English or French' and 'holy meditations': and their way of life influenced the nature of the material they were given. Throughout the Middles Ages, it was more usual for vernacular works to be listened to than read, and we cannot always be sure that either lay patrons or nuns read the works that were written for them rather than hearing them read aloud by someone else; but recluses by definition were solitary readers, and this is sometimes reflected in the works that were provided for their use. In the texts produced for recluses in this period, we see not only the recording in writing of works originally intended for oral delivery, but the development of something still closer to our concept of 'literature,' vernacular works composed with readers rather than hearers in mind.[32]

The English writers studied in this volume are important participants in the movement toward vernacular writing. Indeed, their works have been studied as much by philologists and students of literature, as by those interested in their religious ideas. Whatever their precise motivations for writing in English, their achievement allowed religious treatises to be accessible to new groups of the laity, especially women. Together they represent an important chapter in the development of English vernacular writing generally, and religious writing in particular.

THE FOURTEENTH CENTURY: AN ANXIOUS AGE

Although historians' assessments of the fourteenth century vary, it is impossible to ignore the number of major disasters that occurred within it. Called the 'age of adversity' and 'calamitous',[33] the fourteenth century was one of the blackest in human history in terms of the magnitude of human suffering it produced through 'plague, war, taxes, brigandage, bad government, insurrection, and church schism'. It was, in short, 'a violent, tormented, bewildered, suffering and disintegrating age'.[34]

In England, the century began and ended with the troubled reigns of weak, ineffectual monarchs, Edward II (1307–27) and Richard II (1377–99), both of whom were deposed and murdered by their adversaries. Edward III, who governed throughout the middle of the century (1327–77), was preoccupied with war for most of his reign. Fighting with Scotland was chronic and the conflict with France known as the Hundred Years' War began in 1337. Methods of warfare were in transition, and the butchering, looting, and raping that comprised the 'battles' of the century bore no resemblance to the glorious ideals of chivalry. In the lapses between phases of the war, bands of mercenaries, for want of occupation and funds, plundered the countryside at will, making highways perilous for travellers.

To finance these wars, taxes were levied upon all segments of the population, not excepting the clergy and the poor. Such taxes became increasingly burdensome as the century wore on, especially since governmental and military mismanagement was perceived as responsible for both wasting resources and inglorious defeats on the battlefield. Nobles, landowners, and merchants were sometimes able to protest through parliamentary resistance, which included the impeachment of royally appointed officials. The poor had no such recourse. The notorious poll tax of 1380 proved to be the last straw for the disgruntled peasants of England. It fomented the brief but violent uprising led by Wat Tyler known as the Peasants' Revolt, which succeeded in freeing serfs from prison, executing government officials, burning the houses of noblemen, and ransacking the Tower of London, before an uneasy peace was restored. Much of history is silent about the suffering of the underclasses, but this attempt at revolt gives us a glimpse into the smoldering resentment against the injustices of serfdom and tenancy felt by those on the lowest rungs of English society.

Ominously, the century began with widespread famine throughout Europe, including England. Tales were told of people eating horses, dogs, even other humans, to survive; thousands starved. But this suffering was pale in comparison to what was to come. In 1348 the plague, the notorious Black Death, visited England, returning again in 1361–2, 1368–9, and the 1370s. Although the exact number of fatalities eludes the historian, it is estimated that the population of England may have been cut nearly in half by the end of the century as a result of this scourge.

Apart from the vast numbers of victims involved, the horror of the Black Death was amplified by the gruesome nature of its symptoms and the swiftness of its progress toward death. In the absence of adequate medical knowledge, speculation about the cause of the plague was prone to superstition; some blamed the Jews, others the devil. But the most common conclusion was that the plague had been sent as divine punishment for sin. Pope Clement VI issued a bull in 1348 calling the plague 'the pestilence with which God is afflicting the Christian people.'[35] Likewise, in Langland's *Piers Plowman,* we read, 'Reason preached reverently before the whole realm, And proved that the plague was for sin purely.'[36] Some compared the plague to the great flood of Genesis; others saw it as the end of the world.

One of the horrors of the plague was the fact that many went to their deaths without benefit of the last rites for want of a priest willing or able to assist them. Thus, fear of eternal punishment accompanied the death throes of the plague's victims. It was commonly believed that most sins committed during one's lifetime were deserving of hellfire, and to die deprived of the opportunity to make a final confession was considered the ultimate misfortune. Fourteenth-century preachers had done their work well – a good, robust fear of the possibility of final damnation was deemed beneficial for their hearers.[37]

Confession was by far the most significant sacrament for fourteenth-century England. Long before the onset of the plague, catechetical teaching was preoccupied with the issues of sin and salvation. The reforming Lateran Council of 1215 had made mandatory the annual confession of sins, prescribing instruction for both clergy and laity in the method of hearing and making a good confession. The English bishops were almost overzealous in their efforts to implement the Council, legislating the confession mandate even more rigorously; the faithful were to confess their sins three times annually: at Eastertide, Christmastide, and during the Pentecost season. The penalty for noncompliance could be excommunication, bringing with it the prospect of eternal damnation.[38]

On a more positive note, the English bishops were thorough in making sure the laity were instructed in the fundamentals of Christianity. Instructional manuals were produced, aimed primarily at parish priests, those directly responsible for the instruction of the laity. Archbishop Pechem's *De informatione simplicium,* issued in 1281, laid down the detailed syllabus of religious instruction that would become standard throughout the fourteenth century. Its subject matter, reproduced in countless Latin and vernacular manuals, included the Apostles' Creed, the ten commandments of the law, the two command- ments of the gospel, the seven works of mercy, the seven virtues, the seven deadly sins, and the seven sacraments. These were to be expounded to the laity in the vernacular four times a year. The primary method for such instruction was public preaching, the chief occupation of the Franciscan and Domin- ican friars, which was emulated by clergy of every type and rank. Eventually, some of the Latin manuals were translated into English specifically for the educated laity, often rendered into verse to facilitate memorization. Two popular examples are *Handling Sin* and *The Lay Folk's Catechism*. Such instruc- tion also survives in the secular literature of the period, in Chaucer's 'Parson's Tale', for instance, and in *Piers Plowman*.[39]

The preoccupation with sin, confession, penance, and fear of eternal damnation, already prevalent for over a century, was exacerbated by the Black Death. Some turned to asceticism to appease a wrathful deity. Others succumbed to scepticism: how could one trust religious teachings about a good, just and powerful God, when a disaster of such magnitude could happen for no apparent reason? Many were demoralized and resigned to dissolute living, as witnessed by a telling passage from Lang- land's *Piers Plowman*:

> Friars and fakers have fashioned such questions
> To please proud men with since the plagues,
> And are preaching at Saint Paul's out of pure envy of
> clerics,
> So that the people are not firm in their faith nor free
> with their goods
> Nor sorry for their sins; pride is so enhanced
> In religious orders and in all the realm among rich and
> poor
> That prayers have no power to hinder these plagues.
> For God is deaf nowadays and deigns not to hear us
> And for our guilt grinds good men all up to death.

And yet the wretches of this world are not warned by
  each other,
Nor out of dread of death withdraw from their pride
Nor share with the poor, as pure charity requires,
But in gaiety and in gluttony swallow their goods
And break not their bread with the poor.[40]

The behaviour of the church hierarchy during the century did
little to alleviate this general demoralization. In 1302, partly in
response to illegal practices of clergy taxation practised by
Philip IV of France, Pope Boniface VIII issued the bull *Unam
sanctam,* declaring that salvation was dependent upon sub-
mission to papal authority, both temporal and spiritual. His
successor, the French pope Clement V, set up his court at
Avignon instead of Rome, initiating the so-called 'Babylonian
captivity' of the papacy. The scandalous luxury of the Avignon
court was financed by the selling of church offices, pardons,
dispensations, and indulgences, and by severe taxation.

The popes remained at Avignon until 1377, when, under the
influence of the reforming zeal of Catherine of Siena, Pope
Gregory XI returned to Rome, only to die the following year.
Fearful that another French pope might mean the return of the
papacy to Avignon, the citizens of Rome sent a delegation to
the college of cardinals, demanding that an Italian be chosen
as the next pope. The college elected the Italian Urban VI, who
immediately excoriated his fellow cardinals for their luxurious
lifestyles, and attempted to cut off their sources of income. In
retaliation, the cardinals declared his election invalid on the
grounds that they had been coerced into choosing him by
the Roman mob. In his place they elected a Frenchman,
Clement VII, who set up court again at Avignon. This was
Robert of Geneva, the 'butcher of Cesena' who, in 1377, during
one of the skirmishes to reclaim the papal states, had tricked
the citizens of Cesena into laying down their arms, only to have
them massacred by mercenaries. No one could have been more
distasteful to the citizens of Italy. Catherine of Siena's response
to the cardinals voiced the sentiments of many:

Oh, unhappy men! You who were to nourish yourselves at the breast of the Church, to be as flowers in her garden, to shed forth sweet perfume, to be as pillars to support the Vicar of Christ and his bark, as lamps for the enlightenment of the world and diffusion of the faith ... you who were angels upon earth, have turned to the way of devils ... What is the cause? The poison of selfishness destroys the world.[41]

Urban VI refused to give up the papacy, thus beginning the Great Schism which was to last until 1418. All of Europe was divided, pledging allegiance to whichever pope was deemed the more advantageous ally; people were expected to follow the prince's choice of allegiance. In defiance of France, England allied itself with the Roman pontiff. The effect upon people's faith was disastrous. Since each pope had excommunicated the followers of the other, how could one be sure of salvation? If one's prince had chosen the wrong pope, one's eternal life could be in jeopardy.

Heretical movements presented a problem to the Church throughout the Middle Ages, particularly from the twelfth century on, with the widespread Cathar or Albigensian movement, and subsequently with the Waldensians, the Spiritual Franciscans, and the heretical followers of Joachim of Fiore.[42] With the exception of the Waldensians, all of these movements espoused genuinely heretical teachings. However, their popular appeal lay primarily in their reforming zeal for a simpler, purer Church in place of clerical misconduct and ecclesial abuse of power. Throughout the Middle Ages, concern about unauthorized preaching or teaching by the laity, especially by women, prompted church authorities to investigate them for heresy. In 1231, Pope Gregory IX established the Inquisition for the purpose of seeking out and prosecuting heretics.

Unlike the rest of Europe, England remained free of any organized heretical movement until the late fourteenth century, when the teachings of John Wyclif, an Oxford theologian, were disseminated by his followers to the English

populace at large.[43] Wyclif envisioned a complete overhaul of
the Church, advocating the elimination of hierarchical
authority, the clerical priesthood, religious orders, and popular
devotions such as pilgrimage and the veneration of images. In
place of these he endorsed the authority of Scripture, understood quite literally, and as interpreted by patristic authors,
especially Augustine. He made political friends by calling for
the disendowment of ecclesial lands and possessions and their
redistribution to the laity. Some of Wyclif's teachings were condemned by the pope in 1377, and he was officially barred from
Oxford in 1382. The Lollard movement, fuelled by his ardent
followers, became gradually less academic in tone, focusing on
preaching and disseminating English translations of Scripture
to the laity.

Lollardy was appealing to people, setting fire to 'an old store
of combustible anticlericalism and untapped religious zeal.'[44]
Direct access to Scripture and individual interpretation of its
meaning were attractive options, particularly in the atmosphere created by growing vernacular literacy. The movement
spread rapidly, prosecuted with relative mildness at first, due
in part to the English Church's inexperience with heresy. In
1401 the penalty of death by burning for lapsed heretics was
written into English law, and the first Lollard was burned that
year. To stem the tide of lay access to vernacular religious
writing, Thomas Arundel, Archbishop of Canterbury, issued
his *Constitutions* in 1409, requiring that not only Scripture
translations, but all religious writing in English be submitted
to church authorities for review. Furthermore, such writing
designed for the laity was to be limited to the topics outlined in
Pechem's syllabus. Directed primarily against Lollards, this
regulation was an attempt to censor any speculative thinking
about doctrine among the laity, and had a devastating effect on
the creation of vernacular religious literature in the fifteenth
century.[45] Two rebellions against the secular government, the
first in 1414 (led by Oldcastle) and the second in 1431, caused
the Lollard movement to lose popular support, yet it continued
to have adherents until the Protestant reformation.

In the early fifteenth century Margery Kempe was accused of Lollardy and interrogated several times, but without conviction. *The Cloud* author, Hilton and Julian, all contemporaries of Wyclif, mention heresy in their writings. There is also evidence that Hilton and Julian were concerned with heresy of a different stripe, that of the so-called Free Spirit Movement on the continent, which was vigorously prosecuted throughout the fourteenth century.[46] It was a heresy for which mystics were particularly suspect, since its adherents were said to disregard the sacraments and Christian moral practices once a certain level of holiness was achieved. Unlike other medieval heretical movements, there was no organized group known as Free Spirits, although beguines and their male counterparts, beghards, were often suspected of it. Robert Lerner, author of the definitive study on the Free Spirit, writes tellingly, 'As if their history had been plotted by the Red Queen, heretics of the Free Spirit were condemned before very many of them can be proved to have existed.'[47] There was a great fear of antinomianism on the part of the church hierarchy in the late Middle Ages, which fomented an overzealous search for those guilty of unorthodox teaching and practice.

Such was the 'bad news' of the fourteenth century, earning it the appellation of a calamitous, anxious age. Yet all the news was not grim. People found pockets of happiness, fulfilment, peace, and prosperity within its months and years. One reads *The Canterbury Tales*, for example, and finds a certain equanimity about life, though Chaucer was not loath to express disdain for society's ills in his characteristic satire. Some members of this century turned to God as an antidote to anxiety and despair, finding there a place of comfort, peace, security, and above all, love. These 'lovers of God', as they liked to call themselves, left precious records of the wisdom gained from their experience for the benefit of others. What follows quotes liberally from each, hoping to let each voice be heard in all its uniqueness.

2. THE POET: RICHARD ROLLE

I know no pleasure sweeter than in my heart to sing you a song of praise, Jesus my love ... When first I was converted and became single-minded, I used to think I would be like the little bird which pines for love of its beloved, but which can rejoice in the midst of its longing when he, the loved one, comes. While it sings its joy, it is still yearning, though in sweetness and in warmth. It is said that the nightingale will sing her melody all night long to please him to whom she is united. How much more ought I to sing, and as sweetly as I can, to my Jesus Christ, my soul's spouse, through the whole of this present life ... Flute-like, I shall pour out melodious, fervent devotion, raising from the heart songs of praise ... Good Jesus, bestow on me the rich melody and heavenly song of the angels, so that, enraptured, I may ever chant your praises ... Good Jesus, you have bound my heart to think of your Name, and now I cannot but sing it. So pity me by perfecting what you have planned.

The Fire of Love, chapter 42[1]

The tradition of affective piety, evident in this quotation, has no better representative among the writers considered in this volume than Richard Rolle. He is controversial because of the idiosyncrasy of his lifestyle and the self-preoccupation apparent in some of his writings. Modern critics have not been kind to Rolle, comparing him unfavourably to Walter Hilton and the author of *The Cloud.*[2] However, if we approach him as someone with an artist's soul, self-consciously plying the writer's craft, we may be able to view him more favourably.

In his comprehensive study of Rolle's writings, Nicholas Watson treats Rolle's life as 'a single vast rhetorical construct', through which he developed as a successful spiritual writer.[3] Apart from a few lyrics, Rolle wrote in prose, yet Watson finds Dante a fitting parallel to Rolle. Both lived during a time when 'poetry began to rise to a new consciousness of its own eminence.' Like Dante, Rolle 'presents himself as a modern who is fully the equal to his predecessors.' For Dante these predecessors are the great classical poets like Virgil and Ovid; for Rolle, they are masters of contemplative writing like Bernard of Clairvaux and Richard of St Victor. Like Dante, Rolle is 'intensely aware of his own originality and of the divine inspiration that sustains it.' Both are preoccupied with their careers, engaging in constant reinterpretation of their lives and writings. Such self-preoccupation might seem inappropriate for a pastoral writer concerned with nurturing the spiritual lives of others, but it may be inevitable for one motivated by creative genius to become a great writer. Watson's final assessment is that Rolle deserves to be recognized as a major author 'for the brilliance, resourcefulness and originality of his prose, and for the grandeur of the task he successfully carried out.'[4]

A reason for the defensiveness sometimes present in Rolle's writings has to do with the genre in which he was trying to establish himself as a writer. Unlike Dante, whose models were the secular classical poets, Rolle's models were the mystical masters of the Christian tradition, all of whom enjoyed clerical status. As a layperson, Rolle did not have the credentials to claim authority on religious topics; he needed to 'invent his authority' as Watson puts it, so that his insights into religious experience would be taken seriously.[5]

An assessment of Rolle as a highly gifted, deliberate writer need not mean that he was insincere or dishonest in reporting his religious experience. Nor does it mean that those who approach his works will find nothing there of value for themselves. Such an assessment, however, does help us understand aspects of Rolle's works that have been regarded negatively in the past. Rolle tells us he wanted to sing like the nightingale – 'as sweetly as I can' – to his love, Jesus. This was his life's project and we do him a disservice to ignore it.

ROLLE'S LIFE AND WORK

Rolle is the most prolific of the English mystics; his writings are voluminous and exist in hundreds of manuscripts. He was the most widely read English author of the late Middle Ages, and his popularity continued well into the sixteenth century. Indeed, to this day, certain of his works have never been out of print. After his death in 1349 (possibly from the plague), Rolle was widely regarded as a saint, though no record of a formal application for canonization exists. An office for the celebration of his feast day, *Officium et miracula*, was compiled in the 1380s.[6] Though its hagiographical details are historically untrustworthy, it does provide some rudimentary facts about Rolle's life, beyond which we know little.

Richard Rolle was born at Thornton near Pickering in Yorkshire, the son of William Rolle, an employee of the same John Dalton who later became Rolle's first patron. Rolle studied at Oxford, but left a good two years short of attaining a degree. This meant that he could not be ordained or preach or teach in any official capacity, nor could he receive a benefice which would provide him with a steady income. Instead of entering upon an officially sanctioned ecclesial career, Rolle became a hermit to pursue a life of holiness. Even here, Rolle was a nonconformist. He should have sought permission to undertake the eremitical life from the local bishop, and given some proof of his ability to support himself through work or endowment. There is no evidence that he did anything of the kind.

With his emphasis upon poverty and joy, and his devotion to the Holy Name of Jesus, Rolle's piety exhibits Franciscan influence. In fact, a colourful anecdote associated with Rolle's conversion bears a striking resemblance to the story of the conversion of Francis of Assisi. Like Francis, Rolle flees his father's house; like Francis, who stripped himself of his rich clothing to put on the garb of a beggar, Rolle initiates his new life with a dramatic change of clothing:

> After he had returned from Oxford to his father's house, he said one day to his sister, who loved him with tender affection: 'My beloved sister, thou hast two tunics which I greatly covet, one white and the other gray. Therefore I ask thee if thou wilt kindly give them to me, and bring them me tomorrow to the wood near by, together with my father's rain-hood.' She agreed willingly, and the next day, according to her promise, carried them to the said wood, being quite ignorant of what was in her brother's mind. And when he had received them he straightway cut off the sleeves from the gray tunic and the buttons from the white ... Then he took off his own clothes with which he was clad and put on his sister's white tunic next his skin, but the gray, with the sleeves cut out, he put on over it, and put his arms through the holes which had been cut; and he covered his head with the rain-hood aforesaid, so that ... he might present a certain likeness to a hermit.[7]

This strange garb was a home-made version of the traditional grey and white hermit's habit usually provided in an investing ceremony by the proper ecclesial authority.

Rolle seems never to have been gainfully employed. Given his productivity as a writer, it is hard to see how he could have done much more than pray and write. Instead of working for his living, Rolle sought patrons who would support his hermit's lifestyle, the first of whom was John Dalton, on whose estate Rolle lived for about three years.[8] We do not know where he went after this. Yorkshire, so close to the Scottish border, was sporadically affected by the conflict with Scotland, and Rolle may have needed to move to avoid this. He also may have periodically worn out his welcome with one or another of his patrons, or may have been forced to move because of a change in their economic status. His moves seem to have generated some criticism, for Rolle is defensive about them.[9] By the end of his life, Rolle was living at Hampole near a Cistercian nunnery, possibly acting as a spiritual guide to the nuns there.

Rolle was trained to write in Latin, and this is the language in which he is more adept. His Latin writings succeed better in transmitting the intensity of his feeling, and reproduce more easily the models of style and structure which were his sources. Most of his English writings were composed for a specific person or situation, and are written in a more sober, practical style than his Latin works, which were motivated more directly by his inner compulsion to write. Rolle's writings fall into three general categories: commentaries and meditations on Scripture, treatises or epistles on the spiritual life, and lyric poetry. What follows will examine the first two categories, with a few lyrics included in the discussion.

COMMENTARIES AND MEDITATIONS ON SCRIPTURE

Early in his career, Rolle composed several short Latin commentaries on the creeds, the Lord's Prayer, the Lamentations of Jeremiah, and the book of Revelation, in each case imitating the style of the *Glossa ordinaria*.[10] Two later Latin commentaries, on Psalm 20 (21) and on the beginning verses of the Song of Songs, exhibit more originality. Finally, his *Super lectiones mortuorum (On the Readings for the Dead)*, written much later, is a highly original, verse-by-verse commentary on the passages from Job which form the readings for the divine office for the dead. This is a long sermon-like meditation, consistent with the texts it explicates, on the transitory nature of life on earth, God's anger at sin, and the need for penance in this life to avoid damnation in the next. A theme unsettling to modern ears, it was expounded regularly in the fourteenth century, reflecting the anxiety of the age, and is frequent in Rolle's writings. Its opening lines will suffice as an example:

> *Spare me, Lord, for my days are as nothing* [Job 7:16]. In these words are expressed the instability of the human

condition, which does not have in this vale of anguish any *abiding estate* [Hebrews 13:14]; rather, power will pass from perverse princes, and they without doubt will be thrust into the thickest flames of hell, and the languor of the lascivious will lapse at once in lamentation, because the riches of the affluent and the temples of tyrants will within a short time come to an end. Therefore I announce this to you who delight in a transitory sweetness and long to abound in these earthly riches: that you will have sorrow from your joy, seeing that everything which you gather together under the sun will vanish; your play will turn into pain and your prosperity be changed into torment ... Here I demand, I beg, I implore, I ask: *Spare me, Lord,* so I may not perish with the depraved, not be condemned with the wicked.[11]

Rolle is an excellent example of a mystic rooted in the practice of *lectio divina*. He tells us his own experience of song (*canor*) grew out of the recitation of the psalms:

While I was ... repeating as best I could the night-psalms ... I heard ... the joyful ring of psalmody ... I became aware, in a way I cannot explain, of a symphony of song, and in myself I sensed a corresponding harmony at once wholly delectable and heavenly, which persisted in my mind. Then and there my thinking itself turned into melodious song, and my meditation became a poem, and my very prayers and psalms took up the same sound.[12]

Rolle's love for the psalms remained throughout his life, and he wrote two line-by-line commentaries on the entire book of Psalms, one in Latin and one in English, an amazing achievement by any reckoning. The English version is not a mere translation of his Latin one, although it is partly based on it. The first long biblical commentary ever written in English, it became one of Rolle's most popular works. It is written in the melodic style of Rolle's experience of song, and it is easy to see why people with no access to Latin editions of the Bible would

have gained much fruit from this admirable work.[13] The prologue is designed to attract Rolle's readers to the psalms and to
the desire for the experience of prayerful song they promise:

> A great fullness of spiritual comfort and joy in God comes
> into the hearts of those who recite or devoutly intone the
> psalms as an act of praise to Jesus Christ. They drop
> sweetness in [people's] souls and pour delight into their
> thoughts and kindle their wills with the fire of love,
> making them hot and burning within, and beautiful and
> lovely in Christ's eyes. And those who persevere in their
> devotion he raises up to the life of meditation, and, on
> many occasions, he exalts them to the melody and celebra-
> tions of heaven ... Indeed, this radiant book is a choice
> song in God's presence, like a lamp brightening our life,
> health for a sick heart, honey to a bitter soul ... Now see:
> with wholesome instruction it brings agitated and tem-
> pestuous souls into a fair and peaceful way of life ... The
> song which gives delight to hearts and instructs the soul
> has become a sound of singing: with angels whom we
> cannot hear we mingle words of praising.[14]

The passion of Christ is rarely mentioned in Rolle's earlier
Latin writings, where he seems to regard meditation on the
passion as helpful only to beginners in prayer. But later, Rolle
recommends such meditation for people in any stage of spiritual development.[15] There are two very different passion
meditations, both written in English, attributed to Rolle,
although his authorship of both has been questioned. The first,
Meditation A, is a matter-of-fact listing of each detail of the
passion narratives, inviting the reader to consider Christ's sufferings, but leaving the precise nature of personal application
to the imagination of the reader. The second, *Meditation B*, is
more impassioned and dramatic, written throughout as a
prayer to Jesus, emphasizing gratitude for each of his sufferings and including petitions for specific graces connected to
each.[16] It is reminiscent of the type of meditation used in
modern times for the Stations of the Cross. For example,

Sweet Jesu, I thank you with all my heart for all the blood which you so copiously shed in your crowning in front of all those people, when your sweet face was covered in blood and on every side you were vehemently shouted at and scoffed at and pushed along to that violent and repulsive death, and judged so unjustly to it: may you be blessed and thanked, sweet Jesu, as one deserving of being loved by all creatures. Here, Sweet Jesu, I implore you, wash my soul with that blood and anoint and decorate my soul and my consciousness with that precious blood, and send me the grace, through your great compassion, to judge and criticize myself with full comprehension, so that my soul may be saved.[17]

These meditations obviously belong to the tradition begun by Anselm in the late eleventh century and continued in the highly popular *Meditations on the Life of Christ,* attributed to Bonaventure.

TREATISES AND EPISTLES ON THE SPIRITUAL LIFE

The works for which Rolle is best remembered are those in which he offers guidance for spiritual progress. These writings include the Latin works *Incendium amoris (The Fire of Love), Liber de amore Dei contra amatores mundi (Book of the Love of God against the Lovers of the World), Melos amoris (The Melody of Love), Emendatio vitae (The Mending of Life),* and those in English: *Ego Dormio, The Commandment,* and *The Form of Living.* All belong to the type of instruction which organizes the Christian life into stages of ascent from a lower to a higher form of living. It will be useful to summarize some of the influential continental works in this genre before turning to Rolle's specific contributions to it.

The most basic form of this progression dates back at least to the Pseudo-Dionysius in the sixth century, and was popularized in the Middle Ages by *The Threefold Way* of Bonaventure.[18] It begins with the *purgative way*, or way of penance, in which one experiences conversion from worldly attractions to heavenly things, accompanied by the painful process of rooting out habitual vices and sins. The second step is the *illuminative way*, in which one grows gradually in appreciation for God and the things of God, being instructed in the life of virtue. Finally, the *unitive way* raises one up into contemplative union with God, initiating experiences often difficult to describe in words.

A variation occurs in the type of spiritual instruction which Bernard McGinn calls the 'ordering of charity', founded on the idea that, since God surpasses all human knowing, union with God can be attained only by love. The theme of love became the preoccupation of the spiritual writers of the twelfth century, influenced by the ideal of courtly love sung by the troubadours. Not only could the love of God be experienced and described; it was thought that it could also be set in order, not in an effort to stifle or control it, but to enable it to reach its full potential.[19] Two twelfth-century works in this genre exerted considerable influence on Rolle: Bernard of Clairvaux's *On Loving God* and Richard of St Victor's *Four Degrees of Violent Charity*.

Bernard's *On Loving God* identifies four degrees of love, the first of which is carnal love, wherein a person loves oneself for one's own sake. This most basic degree of love is good, reflecting the fact that humans are made in God's image, thus essentially lovable. But since that image is marred by sin, one needs God's redemptive love to transform preoccupation with self into a desire for spiritual realities. Jesus is the example of the kind of humble and generous love, both for God and others, that humanity is capable of. Rolle echoes Bernard when he sees reflection on the life of Christ, particularly his passion, as the type of meditation most profitable for beginners on the spiritual journey. This type of prayerful reflection initiates one into the second degree of love, whereby a person loves God for one's own sake, for what God can do and has done for one. This stage produces an awareness of the need for God: 'God slowly and gradually becomes known in the form of acquaintance and so grows sweet. In this way, having tasted that the Lord is sweet

[Ps 33:9], the soul passes to the third stage.' In this third degree of love, one loves God no longer for oneself, but for God's sake alone. Bernard anticipated that one would remain at this level for a very long time. The final degree, in which one loves oneself only for God's sake, indicating a completely self-abnegating love, Bernard judged unattainable in this life on earth, save for transitory moments of mystical union.[20]

The second work in this genre known to Rolle is the brief twelfth-century tract *The Four Degrees of Violent Charity*, written by the Augustinian canon, originally from Scotland, Richard of the famous house of St Victor outside Paris.[21] It describes how love leads to union with God and service of one's neighbour, using the erotic language and imagery of courtly love to describe the spiritual journey in four degrees. First, wounding or *insuperable love* pierces the soul, setting it on fire with desire for the Beloved. This is like betrothal, when God's grace inflames the affections, encouraging one to desert the world and its pleasures for the love of Christ (like the purgative way). The second degree of love, binding or *inseparable love*, is akin to the marriage ceremony, when the mind is absorbed with heavenly mysteries (reminiscent of the illuminative way). The third degree of love, languishing or *singular love*, corresponds to sexual consummation, in which the soul is so ecstatically united to Christ that it is melted down and reformed into Christ (similar to the unitive way). Finally, the fourth degree of love, *insatiable love*, causes one to faint or die from a longing for the Beloved which can never be satisfied. The soul therefore passes through a kind of mystical death and is reborn to continue Christ's saving work in the world. This movement is akin to the generativity of sexual union – to bearing children.[22] In Richard's scheme, as in that of the majority of Christian mystics, mystical union is not meant for oneself alone, but is meant to bear fruit for the sake of the community. By including this last degree of insatiable love, Richard determines, like Bernard, that absolute union with God, in any totally absorbing sense, is impossible in this life. Thus one turns one's attention, in imitation of Christ, to the service of one's needy neighbour.

Rolle's own experience can be understood in terms of the threefold way of purgation, illumination and union. In *The Fire of Love* he speaks of the need for conversion, the project of the purgative way, and recounts how this occurred for him: 'As adolescence dawned in my unhappy youth, present too was the grace of my Maker. It was he who curbed my youthful lust and transformed my soul from the depths to the heights, so that I ardently longed for the pleasures of heaven more than I had ever delighted in physical embrace or worldly corruption.'[23]

Once Rolle began living as a hermit after his conversion, his life could be expected to resemble that of the illuminative way, although he tells us little about this phase of his life. Roughly three years after he became a hermit, he experienced what he calls the opening of the heavenly door, which bears some resemblance to experiences typical of the illuminative way. The image reflects Revelation 4:1 ('there in heaven a door stood open') and Rolle's explication of this passage in his commentary on Revelation provides insight into what he meant by using this image:

> When the darkness of the Scriptures is set forth by the Church, it is as though a door into heaven is opened. Or thus: when the devout soul strives perfectly to be purged from uncleannesses, and when it lifts itself upward by continual meditation and prayer, an unusual light suddenly appears and snatches away the amazed mind. And so, in order that he might become a contemplative, and with his heart's eye now cleansed, he is caught up in the sight of heavenly things, a door is opened in heaven . . . and from it descend mellifluous gifts, and secrets are thrown open.[24]

Nearly a year after this, Rolle began to experience heat, sweetness and song, which he associated with mystical union. These three interrelated gifts are Rolle's most original contribution to mystical literature, and are introduced in *The Fire of Love* thus:

I was sitting in a certain chapel, delighting in the sweetness of prayer or meditation, when suddenly I felt within
myself an unusually pleasant heat. At first I wondered
where it came from, but it was not long before I realized
that it was from none of [God's] creatures but from the
Creator himself. It was, I found, more fervent and pleasant
than I had ever known. But it was just over nine months
before a conscious and incredibly sweet warmth kindled
me, and I knew the infusion and understanding of heavenly, spiritual sounds, sounds which pertain to the song of
eternal praise, and to the sweetness of unheard melody.[25]

There is some ambiguity in Rolle's writings about the nature of
such experiences. Later interpreters have tended to read them
literally, as at least partially available to the physical senses.
Others have regarded them as indicative of a lower stage of
spiritual progress, and not appropriate for the unitive way.
However, Rolle probably meant heat, sweetness and song to be
understood as metaphors describing the 'spiritual senses'.[26] As
such, they are no different from the attempts of other mystics
to put into words the ineffable experience of union with God. As
Watson points out, the images Rolle uses are inclusive of all five
spiritual senses: sight (sight into heaven), touch (heat), smell
or taste (sweetness), and hearing (song).[27]

Rolle eventually organized his experience into a general
system describing what people dedicated to a life of contemplation might expect. Summaries of this are found scattered
throughout his works, like this example from *The Fire of Love*:

When a man is perfectly converted to Christ, he will hold
in contempt all things that are transient, but keep a tight
hold on his longing for his Maker . . . And then . . . he sees
with his inward eye *heaven open*, as it were, and all the
inhabitants there. Then it is that he feels that *warmth*
most sweet, burning like a fire. He is filled with wonderful
sweetness, and glories in jubilant *song*. Here indeed is
charity perfected, and no one can know what it is like

unless he lays hold of it; and he who does never loses it, but lives in sweetness and dies in safety.[28]

Ego Dormio,[29] the first of Rolle's works of spiritual instruction written in English, clearly outlines the triple way of purgation, illumination and union, although its stages are called degrees of love: 'The first degree of love occurs when [one] keeps the Ten Commandments and keeps [oneself] from the seven deadly sins and is firm in [one's] faith in holy church, and refuses, for the sake of any earthly matter, to anger God . . . It is essential for everyone who wants to be saved to have this degree of love' (135).

Once one has lived according to the commandments and has rooted out all mortal sins, one is ready for the second degree of love: 'You will . . . give up the whole world, your father and your mother and all your relations, and follow Christ in poverty. In this degree you are to make every effort to be pure in heart and chaste in body and devote yourself to simplicity, endurance and obedience, and see how beautiful you can make your soul in virtue' (136). One is gradually attracted more and more to Jesus: 'You will feel inclined to steal away on your own to think about Jesus and to be in deep prayer, for through good thoughts and holy prayers your heart is to be made burning in the love of Jesus Christ, and then you are bound to feel sweetness and spiritual joy, both in praying and meditating' (137). This is aided by that devotion to the name of Jesus for which Rolle is famous:

> Love this name *Jesus*, and meditate on it in your heart so that you never forget it wherever you are. And, assuredly, I promise you that you will find great joy and strength in it; and because of the love with which you love Jesus so tenderly and as such an intimate friend, you will be filled with grace on this earth and be Christ's beloved maiden and wife in heaven. This is because nothing pleases God so much as true devotion to [the] name of *Jesus*. If you love it properly and enduringly . . . you will be carried away in

ecstasy into a higher life than you know how to wish for.
(137)

Rolle ends his discussion of the illuminative way with a lyric
for the reader's daily meditation. It begins as a typical meditation on Christ's passion:

My king much water wept and much blood he let;
And was most sorely beat till his own blood ran wet,
When their scourges met. Most hard they did then fling
And at the pillar swing; his dear face smeared with
    spitting. (138)

After continuing in this vein for several verses, the tone of the
poem changes to a deeply felt expression of love and longing for
union with God, ending thus:

[Save you, I yearn for nought; this world therefore] I flee;
You are what I have sought; your face I long to see.
You make my soul most bright, as love can alter sight.
How long must I be here? [When may I come you near]
Your melody to hear, of love to hear the song
Which is enduring long? [Will] you be my loving
That I your love may sing? (139)

Clearly, Rolle believes that the most appropriate type of meditation for those on the illuminative way is focused on the
human Jesus, especially on his passion. He is convinced that
such meditation, if faithfully pursued, will eventually initiate
one into the heights of contemplation and the third degree of
love.

In the third degree of love, Rolle's reader is counselled that
she, like he, will enjoy the mystical gifts of heat, sweetness and
song:

When you first reach it, your spiritual eye is carried up into
the glory of heaven and there is enlightened by grace and
set ablaze by the fire of Christ's love in your heart, constantly lifting your mind toward God, [filling you full of]
love, joy and sweetness ... And then, because of the elev-

ation of your heart [your] prayers turn into joyful song and your thoughts into sweet sounds. Then Jesus is all your desire, all your delight, all your joy, all your consolation, all your strength [so that] your song will always be about him, and in him all your rest. Then you may indeed say: 'I sleep and my heart wakes. Who shall to my lover say that for his love I long always?' (140)

Rolle's indebtedness to the tradition of the ordering of charity is evident in his calling the steps of spiritual progress degrees of love. His indebtedness to the tradition of bridal mysticism is also evident in *Ego Dormio*, particularly in the opening section, where he presents himself as a mediator between the nun for whom he writes and her would-be bridegroom, Christ:

Because I love [you] I am courting you in order to have you exactly as I would wish – not for myself, but for my lord! I want to become [a] go-between to lead you to the bed of the one who has set you up and paid for you, Christ, son of the king of heaven, because he is eager to [marry] you if you are willing to give him your love. (133)

Bernard of Clairvaux and Richard of St Victor are Rolle's exemplars for his efforts to combine the courtly love tradition with the experience of contemplation. He learns from them the paradox inherent in the term 'ordered love', for love by its nature is passionate and violent, resisting efforts at rigid ordering. Such paradox is perhaps best represented in Rolle's image of spiritual song – song that is ordered (through rhyme, rhythm, alliteration), but also rhapsodic, always resisting and transcending any order imposed upon it. As such, it is a fitting metaphor for the mystical experience of loving union with God, which always eludes human efforts to express it adequately in words.[30]

Rolle's indebtedness to both Bernard and Richard is evident in direct quotations from their writings, usually unacknowledged, found throughout his works. But he also departs from them both in significant ways. He disagrees with Bernard's point that the fourth degree of love is unable to be sustained by anyone in this life. Rolle uses Bernard's images to describe mystical union in *The Form of Living*:

> We must strive to clothe ourselves in love, as iron or charcoal do in fire, as the air does in the sun, and as the wool does in the dye. The charcoal is so imbued with fire that the whole is fire; [the air so clothes itself in the sun that the whole is light;] the wool so essentially adopts the dye that it [totally] matches it.

But Rolle then links these images to his own favourite image of the fire of love, intimating, in disagreement with Bernard, that such a degree of love is indeed possible in this life: 'In this fashion a real lover of Christ is to act: his or her heart is to burn in love to such an extent that it will be turned into a fire of love, and be, so to speak, entirely fire, and he or she will so shine in virtues that no part of Christ's lover will be darkened by degenerative behavior.'[31]

Rolle considers the heavenly reward awaiting the just in terms of their spiritual progress on earth; they will be admitted into the nine choirs of angels according to the degree of love they have attained on earth. The highest order, the seraphim, is the rank reserved for those who have attained the highest degree of love: 'The word *seraphim* means "burning" and to this order are admitted those who want least from this world and, feeling most sweetness in God, have hearts which are most burning in his love.'[32] The image of the seraphim also allows Rolle to link the image of 'burning' to that of song, for the seraphim eternally sing out the love with which they are aflame before the throne of God. But Rolle also implies that people who have achieved the highest degree of love on earth already participate in some way in the song of the seraphim. They enter into Bernard's fourth degree of love now, being transformed into Christ. They are thus 'deified' and enjoy union with God continuously, like the seraphim:

> For while we unceasingly and indefatigably desire our

Creator alone with all our hearts, . . . we fly up rejoicing, overshadowed by the heat of the light eternal, snatched away by Christ, to the joyfulness of song. And because this song of eternal love is not with us hurriedly and momentarily, but continually, we are not shaken by any adversity or prosperity; we rejoice not rarely but continually.[33]

It is obvious here, through the use of first person pronouns, that Rolle counts himself as one of the privileged lovers of God who has reached Bernard's fourth degree of love. In claiming this for himself, he suggests that he has surpassed Bernard, who never made such a claim for himself, nor did he think such experience possible in this life.

In his discussion of the degrees of love, Rolle frequently uses Richard of St Victor's terminology of *insuperable, inseparable* and *singular love*, although he never clarifies exactly how these correspond to his own pattern of spiritual growth.[34] He ignores Richard's fourth stage of *insatiable love*, where the human lover turns from unsatisfied longing for God back to the world, expressing that longing in service towards others. In *The Mending of Life*, Rolle inserts Richard's degrees of love into the place where he would ordinarily speak of his own experiences of heat, sweetness and song. At first he follows Richard closely, but when he discusses singular love, he directly contradicts his source. Richard says the singular lover longs for God so violently that 'his flesh fails and his heart is consumed'; Rolle claims the lover 'does not fail in his body, nor does his heart weaken' but he 'continues to feel greater love as long as he lives.' This becomes the main theme for what follows, where Rolle's images of heat and song appear: 'The lover of Christ . . . directs his love towards God more and more burningly and joyfully.'[35] Rolle ignores Richard's fourth degree of love and seems to be insisting, as with Bernard, that he has experienced love in a way surpassing that of Richard of St Victor. His experience of union with God is not debilitating nor fleeting nor insatiable, but deeply satisfying, and constantly growing in intensity.

Rolle may have avoided Richard's fourth degree of love because of his tendency to link degrees of perfection with certain states of life: the purgative way (first degree of love) to the active life, the illuminative way (second degree of love) to the contemplative life lived in community, and the unitive way (third degree of love) to the eremitic life. Rolle lived in an atmosphere which generally considered eremiticism the highest form of religious life. This doubtless influenced his decision to abandon an ecclesial career in orders, to reject the possibility of joining a contemplative monastic community, and to adopt the life of a hermit. Richard of St Victor's fourth degree of love does not have a place here, since it seems to be the abandonment of a higher form of living to return to a lower, active life in the world.

However, there was another movement in Rolle's milieu which became important to him later in life. Under the influence of the mendicant orders, a life dedicated to preaching began to rival eremiticism as the highest form of religious life. In fact, preaching was sometimes placed on a par with martyrdom and virginity: martyrs overcome the world, virgins the flesh, but preachers, through their persuasive words, win souls away from the devil. Like martyrs and virgins, they will be rewarded with the aureole or golden crown in heaven.[36] Much was expected of preachers. Besides adequate learning and purity of life (which included both celibacy and single-heartedness), they were expected to be zealous for the salvation of souls.

The term 'mixed life' best describes the lifestyle of the preacher, combining as it does both contemplation and action. In Langland's *Piers Plowman*, the allegorical characters Dowel, Dobet and Dobest represent the active, contemplative and mixed lives, respectively.[37] Langland links the mixed life with that of bishops, one of whose primary duties was preaching. The charism of the Augustinian canons, to whom Richard of St Victor belonged, combined active ministry with a contemplative life lived in common. Richard's advocating service to the world as the aftermath of the experience of contemplative union with God is completely consistent with their view of the mixed life.

To the end of his life, Rolle remained convinced that the solitary life was the most perfect form of religious living, and most conducive to mystical contemplation. As a layperson, he did not qualify for the public, ecclesially regulated office of preaching reserved to the clergy. Nevertheless, he found a way to adopt a form of the mixed life which would enable him to strive for the preacher's aureole. In *The Melody of Love*, Rolle claims that 'the abundance of love urges me to dare to unveil eloquence for the informing of others . . . I do not know how to be silent: so charity constrains me.'[38] The Holy Spirit of Love acts as Rolle's muse, inspiring him to eloquence, much in the same way that *Amor*, personified Love, urged the troubadours to sing, and that Beatrice inspired Dante.

Rolle's method of preaching differs from that of the mendicants. As a solitary dedicated to a life of contemplation, he could not move about from town to town. His preaching comes through his writings which teach others about the wealth of Scripture and exhort them to a life of holiness modelled on his own. Rolle ignores any technical distinction between teaching and preaching. This way of understanding his vocation to preach allows him to regard the solitary life as the highest form of religious living, yet include preaching as an appropriate element within it. The experience of song, which marked the peak of his own mystical experience, is not merely something to be enjoyed privately in personal prayer, but is meant to be sung out to the world. Furthermore, Rolle is convinced that preachers like himself, whose words are grounded in contemplative experience, are those most adequately prepared to speak of the things of God to others. A passage from *The Melody of Love* summarizes Rolle's thoughts on this subject:

> This desert [of the solitary life] is not dreadful to the ardent lover; . . . in quiet he kindles with consuming charity <like a> burning coal. Perfected as a preacher, he brings forth boys to bear peace, and will capture crowns in

the presence of the Omnipotent for converting captives . . .
He will receive a decorous diadem . . . It is good to be a
preacher, to run about, to move, to become tired for the
salvation of souls; but it is better, it is more secure, it is
sweeter to be a contemplative, to feel in advance the
eternal sweetness, to sing the delights of eternal love and
to be snatched in the praise of the Creator by the infusion
of song in jubilation. However, whoever can obtain both
will be the more praiseworthy – yet this will not occur
unless someone becomes a contemplative before becoming
a preacher . . . For whoever desires to rejoice in the excel-
lence of the great name must first make himself a friend of
God, lest perchance he be made the master of error. The
humble, the obedient, the chaste, the merciful, the patient,
and above all the fervent in love receive this gift, who seek
it not for their own glory but for the divine.[39]

In his writings, Rolle continues to ignore Richard of St Victor's
fourth degree of love, and to disagree with its motivation for
turning back to the world. Yet Rolle does, in fact, engage in a
similar version of the mixed life. He probably owes to Richard
the phrase 'he brings forth boys' (*pueros parturit*), which is
similar to Richard's 'bearing of offspring' (*puerperium*) which
occurs in the fourth degree of love. For both, the image of
bearing children is a metaphor for apostolic activity as the fruit
of mystical union with God.

Consequently, Rolle's later works can be read as genuine
efforts at evangelization. His proclaiming the truths of Scripture, as well as the lessons of his own experience, is his way of
engaging in the pastoral ministry of preaching. Four of these
works, in particular, are Rolle's finest, most mature writings.
Missing from them is the self-consciousness that occasionally
mars his early writing. They are written in a plainer, more
moderate, yet still lyrical prose style, and are better organized
than his earlier works. They express a genuine personal
warmth and solicitude on Rolle's part for the individuals to
whom they are addressed. This is true of *Ego Dormio*, discussed

briefly above, and especially of *The Form of Living*, written for
Margaret Kirkeby, with whom Rolle obviously shared a close
friendship. *The Commandment* was written for a nun of
Hampole, possibly also for Margaret Kirkeby, although in a
more restrained style. To these three English works can be
added Rolle's last Latin work, *The Mending of Life* (*Emendatio
vitae*), probably written for William Stopes, a young man in a
religious community.[40]

The Mending of Life is a fitting text with which to end this
discussion of Rolle's works of spiritual instruction. In it Rolle
refrains from identifying the higher privileges of contemplation
with the solitary life, and instead sets his teaching within the
wider compass of Christian instruction in the life of grace. Its
overarching metaphor is a ladder of twelve steps, each of which
occupies a separate chapter of the work.[41] The steps in order
are: conversion, contempt for the world, poverty, the organiz-
ation (or rule) of life, tribulation, patience, prayer, meditation,
reading, purity of mind, the love of God, and contemplation.
Together they mark the steps of the journey from conversion to
contemplation based on Rolle's own experience of life as a
hermit. However, Rolle omits any overtly autobiographical
detail, and adapts the steps of spiritual progress to his non-
eremitic readers, conceding that a similar life of holiness is
possible for everyone.

In the chapters concerned with the purgative way, we get
a glimpse of the moderation typical of the English mystical
tradition. Rolle emphasizes that true conversion ought not to
be motivated negatively by fear of hell, but positively by attraction to Christ. Penitential practices in themselves are not
enough to sustain one in turning away from the world to the
love of God. Recognizing that few of those for whom he writes
will be able to abandon everything for a strict life of poverty,
Rolle speaks of poverty as an inner attitude of mind: 'When [the
gospel] says "Go and sell," think of the exchange of desires
and thoughts, so that [one] who is proud before now becomes
humble.'[42] He emphasizes the need for detachment from possessions, and for avoiding distractions caused by worldly

pursuits, so as to cultivate the habit of prayer and meditation. He includes a list of sins of thought, word and deed, along with remedies for each, in a manner similar to medieval preaching manuals in the penitential genre. But he counteracts these with strong warnings against excessive abstinence or other rigid ascetical practices. Overall, the emphasis is on a positive view of self-discipline motivated not by any hatred of self, but by love for Christ and the desire to be conformed to him.

Chapters 7 to 9 articulate ideas familiar to us by now: Rolle's commitment to the practice of *lectio divina*, the prayerful reading of Scripture, especially the psalms, and to meditation on its message, especially that of the life and passion of Christ, which strengthens one against temptation and enkindles love for Christ. He gives practical advice about turning to prayer in time of temptation, and staying with experiences of consolation as long as they last, but also maintaining constancy in prayer when consolation is absent. Rolle is convinced that these practices will initiate one into a truly virtuous life, wherein one's whole mind will be focused on God and the things of God. One then grows in the love of God and is ready to receive the mystical gifts of heat, sweetness and song. Rolle studiously avoids any statements about who is capable of reaching these gifts. But in his words 'Every true contemplative loves solitude' we can ascertain that he has not changed his opinion about which form of life is most conducive to contemplation.

3. THE DIONYSIAN: THE AUTHOR OF *THE CLOUD OF UNKNOWING*

> When you first begin to undertake [the exercise of contemplation], all that you find is a darkness, a sort of cloud of unknowing; you cannot tell what it is, except that you experience in your will a [naked intent] to God. This darkness and cloud is always between you and your God, no matter what you do, and it prevents you from seeing him clearly by the light of understanding in your reason, and from experiencing him in sweetness of love in your affection. So set yourself to rest in this darkness as long as you can, always crying out after him whom you love. For if you are to experience him or to see him at all, insofar as it is possible here, it must always be in this cloud and in this darkness.
>
> *The Cloud of Unknowing*, chapter 4[1]

It would be difficult to imagine an account of mystical experience, as evidenced in the above quotation, more different from Rolle's descriptions of heat, sweetness and song. The anonymous author of *The Cloud of Unknowing* presents the greatest contrast to Rolle of all the English mystics in temperament, outlook and style. While Rolle's description of the highest contemplative experience is redolent with sensual imagery, that of *The Cloud* is devoid of such imagery. Instead, reaching the heights of contemplative union means leaving all behind, all sensual feeling, all images, all thoughts and ideas, even holy ones, in order to encounter the incomprehensible mystery of God with nothing save the 'naked intent' of the will.

The Cloud and Rolle's writings represent two contrasting

types of mystical experience, frequently denoted by the terms 'apophatic' and 'cataphatic', indicating different ways of experiencing God, each of which illustrates an important aspect of the mystery of God for Christians. The apophatic way is negative, devoid of images, reflecting God's essential unknowability to the human intellect. The cataphatic way is positive and image-filled, reflecting the revelatory nature of all created things as they witness to their Creator, and, most importantly for Christians, reflecting the incarnation of God in Jesus. Every authentic Christian mystical experience must contain some element of both if it is to be true to these essential mysteries of God's incomprehensibility (God's transcendence) and God's revelation of self in creation and incarnation (God's immanence). However, various individuals may emphasize one over the other in their practice or description of mystical contemplation.[2] There has been a tendency, especially since the time of that great explicator of the apophatic way, John of the Cross (1542–91), to consider apophatic mysticism far superior to cataphatic mysticism, although this is questioned by students of spirituality today. Such an assessment has doubtless influenced the judgement that Rolle is inferior to *The Cloud* author with respect to mystical experience. In what follows we will find that, however different Rolle's writings and those of *The Cloud* author appear to be at first sight, they share much in common in their grounding in the Christian spiritual tradition.

THE AUTHOR

Who was the author of *The Cloud of Unknowing* and its related treatises? This vexing question still has no definitive answer.[3] However, James Walsh has made a plausible case that he was a Carthusian priest, a member of that unique order founded in 1084 by Bruno of Cologne, which attempted a marriage between the eremitic and cenobitic forms of religious life. While the monks came together for morning and evening prayer, mass, and occasional meals, the communal nature of their life was down-played in favour of the eremitic ideal. For the most part, the monks lived alone in separate cells, where each maintained a solitary regimen of private prayer and study. They valued learning highly, insisting that each cell be equipped with writing materials, and allowing books, 'the eternal food of our souls', to be taken from the common library to individual cells for private study. The Carthusians regarded such scholarly work as their way of participating in the ministry of preaching (possibly the source for Rolle's inspiration): 'since we cannot preach the Word of God with our mouths, we may do so with our hands', i.e., by writing.[4] However, it was customary for them to publish their writings anonymously, which lends support to the thesis that *The Cloud* author was a Carthusian.[5]

The first English community of Carthusians was established in 1178, and an English Province in 1368. Walsh suggests that the author of *The Cloud* may have been one of three monks from the Beauvale Charterhouse in Nottinghamshire who joined three members from the London house to found the Coventry Charterhouse in 1375. As a native of Nottinghamshire, he would have written in the dialect identified by Phyllis Hodgson as that of 'the north part of the central East Midlands'.[6] Walsh also concludes that the young man to whom *The Cloud* is addressed was probably a Carthusian, for whom the author served as spiritual director.[7]

Hodgson describes *The Cloud* author as 'a skilled theologian and wise director of souls', whose style 'reflects a forceful quizzical personality, tough-minded and down-to-earth, with shrewd insight into psychological difficulties, unsentimental, objective, and austere'.[8] He exhibits a keen, ironic and wry sense of humour, irritation with religious affectation, and a boundless energy and enthusiasm for his topic. The subject matter of *The Cloud* is admittedly difficult, and its practice even more so, but the book is written in such a clear, direct style with the use of concrete images and no technical jargon, that the exercise of apophatic contemplation seems attainable for those who feel called to leave discursive meditation behind.[9]

Besides *The Cloud of Unknowing*, its author wrote several

other works, including three 'translations'[10] and three original treatises in epistolary form. According to Walsh's arrangement, *The Cloud* was written first, in the last quarter of the fourteenth century. The other works followed in this order: *Denis's Hidden Theology*, a rendering of the *Mystical Theology* of Pseudo-Dionysius; *The Assessment of Inward Stirrings*, an epistolary treatise on discernment written to a different addressee from that of *The Cloud*; *The Pursuit of Wisdom*, a précis of Richard of St Victor's *Benjamin minor*; *Discernment of Spirits*, an elaboration of two sermons by Bernard of Clairvaux from his *De diversis* (*On Various Topics*); and finally, two letters to the same addressee as *The Cloud*: *A Letter on Prayer* and *A Letter of Private Direction* (also known as *The Book of Privy Counseling*).[11] All were written for the instruction of those desiring to grow in contemplation, and, taken together, help situate a proper understanding of *The Cloud*.

THE DIONYSIAN INFLUENCE

The Cloud author was a medieval Dionysian, influenced by the enigmatic, anonymous Syrian monk of the late fifth or early sixth century who wrote under the pseudonym of Dionysius of Athens, the Areopagite, converted by Paul in Acts 17:34. He was also identified with St Denis, Bishop of Paris, and because this version of his name is the one favoured by *The Cloud* author, I will call him 'Denis' here.[12] Denis authored four brief but dense treatises on theological topics which had immense influence on the subsequent development of theology. The first three of these describe the cataphatic outpouring of God's revelation into human history and humanity's appropriation of that divine fecundity for its return to union with the One from whom all things have come.[13] *The Divine Names* lists the multiplicity of ways God can be imaged or named, through which human orientation to and praise of God is ordered and perfected. The next two treatises explore the beauty of the created order as it continually praises God, *The Celestial Hierarchy* focusing on the orders of angels, and *The Ecclesiastical Hier-*

archy on the Church, particularly its liturgical rites. Such sacraments or 'sacred symbols' are the 'stamps', the 'impressions', the 'perceptible tokens' of the 'invisible things' of God.[14]

The text for which Denis is best remembered, his *Mystical Theology*, is an innocuous looking work because of its brevity, but is extremely powerful in its profundity.[15] Its topic is the return to God through the darkness of unknowing, wherein human reason reaches its limit in face of the mystery of God. A poetical prayer at the beginning of this masterpiece of mystical literature provides a sense of the focus of the work:

> Trinity!! Higher than any being, any divinity, any
>   goodness!
> Guide of Christians in the wisdom of heaven!
> Lead us up beyond unknowing and light,
>   up to the farthest, highest peak of mystic scripture,
>   where the mysteries of God's Word
>   be simple, absolute and unchangeable
>   in the brilliant darkness of a hidden silence.
> Amid the deepest shadow
>   they pour overwhelming light
>   on what is most manifest.
> Amid the wholly unsensed and unseen
>   they completely fill our sightless minds
>   with treasures beyond all beauty.[16]

The predominant scriptural image of the *Mystical Theology* is the account of Moses' ascent of Mount Sinai described in Exodus 19–20.[17] Denis describes this ascent, which is paradigmatic for the human journey toward God, in terms of the threefold way of spiritual development. 'Moses is commanded to submit first to purification and then to depart from those who have not undergone this' (the purgative way). Moses then 'hears the many voiced trumpets' and 'sees the many lights, pure and with rays streaming abundantly;' he 'pushes ahead to the summit of the divine ascents', where he contemplates not God's self, but only God's dwelling place, 'the holiest and highest of the things perceived with the eye of the body or the mind.' All of this is reminiscent of experiences of the illuminative way, through which God's 'unimaginable presence is shown.' But then Moses enters into the unitive way, where he

> breaks free ... of what sees and is seen, and he plunges into the truly mysterious darkness of unknowing. Here, renouncing all that the mind may conceive, wrapped entirely in the intangible and the invisible, he belongs completely to [the One] who is beyond everything. Here, being neither oneself nor someone else, one is supremely united by a completely unknowing inactivity of all knowledge, and knows beyond the mind by knowing nothing.[18]

The author of *The Cloud* knew this work well. Its phrase 'the darkness of unknowing' became 'the cloud of unknowing', the title of his most famous work. He adopted Denis's language and imagery and used them liberally in his own spiritual treatises. He produced his own translation of the work into Middle English, *Denis's Hidden Theology*. However, even a cursory comparison of this translation with its source reveals a significant difference between the two. At the end of the opening prayer to the Trinity cited above, *The Cloud* author prays that he may reach beyond 'all these things ... beyond the reach of mind' (so far consistent with Denis), but then adds *'with affection above mind'* (my emphasis).[19] Similarly, when he describes Moses' leaving behind the illuminative way, he says Moses 'is detached from the intelligible active powers of his soul and from the objects of those powers' (so far following Denis), but then we read, 'It was at this point that Moses, *exercising his affection alone,* ... entered ... into the darkness of unknowing' (my emphasis).[20] In both cases the addition of the affective power of the soul alters Denis's understanding of the mystical way. For Denis, mystical union occurs at the point where reason reaches its absolute limit and gives itself over into the mystery of God. In *The Cloud* author's version, another power of the soul, affection (love or will), replaces reason, thereby allowing one to enter into union with the divine.

This dichotomy between reason and love in the search for union with God is explained clearly by *The Cloud* author in *The Assessment of Inward Stirrings*:

> For if God is your love and your intent, the choice and the ground of your heart, this is enough for you in this life; even though you never see more of him with the eye of reason all your life long. Such a blind shot with the sharp arrow of a love that longs can never miss the bull's-eye, which is God. He himself says in the Book of Love, where he is speaking to a soul languishing with love: ... 'You have wounded my heart [with] one of your eyes' [Song of Songs 4:9]. There are two eyes of the soul, reason and love. By reason we may search out how mighty, how wise, and how good God is in his creatures, but not in himself. But whenever reason falls short, then it is love's pleasure to look alive and to learn to occupy itself. For by love we can find him, experience him, and reach him as he is in himself.[21]

Denis would never have penned such words. For their source, we must look to the same Cistercian and Victorine influences which affected Richard Rolle. For example, Bernard of Clairvaux writes, 'The soul has two eyes. One by which it understands, the other by which it investigates. And of these two, the right eye is love, which wounds by its penetrating search' (*Tract on Charity* 3:16). Richard of St Victor also considered the eye of reason as that which contemplates earthly things, but the eye of love as that which contemplates the things that are above: 'The Savior comes to open the eye whose object is heavenly things ... the contemplation and desire of our salvation. You have wounded my heart, O soul, whom I chose as spouse when I joined you to me in the oneness of love and will' (*Explication of the Canticle* 27).[22] *The Cloud* author has read Denis's *Mystical Theology* in the atmosphere of the 'ordering of charity' created by the twelfth-century Cistercians and Victorines.

Denis's Hidden Theology was translated, not from the original Greek, but from the Latin of John Sarracenus.[23] However, the author also acknowledges a direct Victorine influence: 'In translating it I have given not just the literal meaning of the text, but, in order to clarify its difficulties, I have followed to a great extent the renderings of the Abbot of St. Victor, a noted and erudite commentator on the same book.'[24] This abbot was Thomas Gallus of the Victorine Abbey of Vercelli, who wrote two commentaries on Denis's *Mystical Theology* in the thirteenth century.[25] Gallus's reading of Denis involved a shift from the supremacy of the intellect to that of the affective properties of the soul, which makes his description of apophatic experience quite different from that of Denis. For Denis, apophatic experience is entirely intellectual.[26] Since the created universe, hierarchically arranged, reveals the Creator, the mind first 'knows' God through the cataphasis of creation. But as it ascends this hierarchy, from the lower to the higher levels of created reality, the mind gradually casts aside this 'knowledge' through a series of negations until it finds itself in the absolute darkness of unknowing, where it passes out of itself (*ecstasis*), giving itself over into the darkness of union with the Light, experiencing the vision of the One. It is true that Denis uses the word *eros* to describe the impelling force behind this intellectual ascent. But this *eros*, this passion and yearning for the vision of the One, is the *eros* of knowing. The dialectic of knowing and unknowing takes place entirely within the intellect until it submits itself in silence to the divine mystery.

Gallus's notion of the journey to God is different from this.[27] He uses the nine-fold structure of the choirs of angels from Denis's *Celestial Hierarchy* to describe the soul's ascent, something Denis himself does not do. Each order of the angels is an analogy for the various stages the soul passes through in its journey toward union with God. Along the way the intellectual and affective powers of the soul proceed together, being gradually purified. But at the eighth stage, the order of the cherubim, the intellect reaches its limit. Beyond this is the order of the seraphim, where the will steps out on its own and enters alone into the darkness of God:

> [The order of the seraphim] contains the highest aspir-
> ations for God, the excesses and inflowings which go
> beyond understanding, burning brilliance and brilliant
> burnings; understanding cannot be drawn into the sublime
> ecstasies of these lights, but only the supreme love which
> can unite . . . This rank embraces God and is wrapped in
> the embraces of the bridegroom . . . In this order the bed is
> laid for the bridegroom and the bride.[28]

For Gallus, 'apophasis begins where *intellectus* ends . . . Love
shuts the door on understanding before it proceeds on to the
mystic darkness.' The affective powers of the soul are thus
superior to the intellect for the pursuit and attainment of union
with God. The cloud of unknowing becomes a metaphor 'not of
self-transcendent intellect, but of its simple abandonment.'[29]
The Cloud author follows Gallus's lead, minus most of the
erotic language, in teaching that love replaces reason as the
power of the soul open to union with God.

There may also have been a Carthusian connection to *The
Cloud* author's study of Denis. The Carthusian Hugo de Balma
wrote a commentary on Denis's *Mystical Theology* at the end of
the thirteenth century, entitled variously *Mystical Theology,
The Road to Zion Mourns* (*Viae Syon lugent*), or *The Threefold
Way to Wisdom* (*De triplici via ad sapientiam*). Following
Gallus, de Balma replaces Denis's pure apophatic failure of
reason with 'the reaching out in love to God, impelled by the
desire of love.'[30]

Walsh concludes that all of these 'medieval Dionysians' succeeded in 'investing an apophatic Neoplatonism with Christian
devotion.'[31] This can be seen in a positive light, giving Denis's
teaching 'a warmer and more affective bent' in which the heart
as well as the intellect is purified by the work of grace.[32] But
there is also a negative effect of this modification of Denis. It
encourages the abandonment of reason in the interest of union
with God in love, opening the door to voluntarism and anti-
intellectualism.[33] After the time of *The Cloud* author, such a
move helped to deepen the undesirable split between theology

and spirituality. Theology, as an intellectual pursuit, begins to be seen as a hindrance rather than a help to the spiritual experience of God, far different from the traditional notion that faith inevitably seeks deeper understanding. The medieval English mystics have frequently been labelled 'anti-intellectual', a charge which is misleading in its exaggeration of what one actually finds in them. But there is in *The Cloud* author a genuine tendency to debase the role of reason in the pursuit of mystical union with God.

In *The Cloud* there is also an emphasis on personal interiority, suggesting that the way to union with God demands withdrawal from the praise of God found in creation and the Church's communal liturgy. Denis's mystical climb involves negation, but it is done within the milieu of the cataphatic expressions of God's revelation in the world and the liturgical life of the Church. One is not told by Denis to withdraw from them in order to get in touch with 'the naked intent of the will', which alone can lead adequately to union with God. Along with an incipient anti-intellectualism there is a tendency toward privatism in *The Cloud*. The author himself would be quite surprised at such charges, but the move has been made for later interpreters to take his ideas in undesirable directions.[34]

THE CLOUD OF UNKNOWING: SUMMARY OF TEACHING

The Cloud of Unknowing consists of a prologue and seventy-five brief chapters. Its topics are discussed somewhat randomly, suggesting that the author wrote ideas down as they occurred to him, rather than working from an overarching plan. His basic project of offering instruction in the practice of apophatic contemplation is informed by practical common sense and down-to-earth advice. In spite of the exalted nature of his topic, one finds no ecstatic flights of fancy here, no erotic raptures, but only simple guidelines for how to dispose oneself to receive the grace of God. As a result, the desire for contemplative union with God and its pursuit sound like the most natural things in the world.

This does not mean that *The Cloud* author meant his book for everyone. The prologue warns it is only for those called to 'the highest point which a perfect soul in this present life can possibly reach, with the help of grace' (101). It is meant for those living the contemplative life, with the possible exception of someone in the active life 'enabled by an abundance of grace to share in the work of contemplation at the highest level . . . now and then' (103).[35] *The Cloud* is thus not a treatise outlining the entire scope of the spiritual life, but is restricted to a type of prayer proper to the unitive way.

However, the author presupposes that those who tackle his book will have prepared themselves for contemplation by practising 'the virtues and exercises of the active life' (102). These would include the practice of *lectio divina* (chapter 35), meditation on the life of Christ, participation in the sacramental life of the Church (the sacrament of penance is mentioned specifically in chapters 15, 16, 28, 31, 35, and 75), being guided by a spiritual director, and living a virtuous life. These cataphatic experiences are a necessary foundation for the author's apophatic way. It would be a serious distortion of the intent of *The Cloud* author to read the text as a negation of the ordinary communal life of Christianity.

Like Rolle and most of his contemporaries, *The Cloud* author holds a hierarchical view of the various stages of the Christian life: the *ordinary* for laypeople in the world, the *special* for clerics and monastics, the *singular* for solitaries, and the *perfect*, which can begin by grace here, but is fulfilled only in heaven. A person usually progresses from one to another, and the author judges that his addressee has moved through the ordinary and special states to the singular one, where he will enter into the solitary life and 'learn to lift up the foot of your love, and step outwards towards that state and degree of life that is perfect, the last state of all' (1:117). Later the author describes two kinds of lives, the active and the contemplative, each of which is divided into a lower and higher level. In the lower part of the active life, which corresponds to the ordinary life of most Christians, one is principally concerned with practising the corporal works of mercy and of charity. In the higher degree of the active life and the lower degree of the contemplative life, one engages in spiritual meditations, particularly on Christ's passion, considers one's sinfulness, and glories in the gifts of God in creatures with thankfulness and praise. Finally, the higher level of the contemplative life introduces one into the experience of darkness, the cloud of unknowing, where one's appropriate attitude is simply 'a loving impulse and a dark gazing into the simple being of God himself alone' (8:136–7).[36]

In order to reach the higher part of the active life, one must, at least for a time, leave behind the activities of the lower part. Similarly, if one is called to engage in the higher part of the contemplative life, one must leave behind the practices of the lower part. *The Cloud* author uses this division to explain why it is necessary to put aside all images, thoughts, and feelings, no matter how holy they might be in themselves, or how appropriate for another stage of life, in order to enter into the dark cloud of unknowing. The author's apophaticism is therefore not a denigration of cataphatic experiences as such, but a temporary abandonment of them during the exercise of imageless contemplation.

The Cloud emphasizes the arduous, often burdensome nature of the 'exercise' of apophatic contemplation, and constantly encourages perseverance in the 'effort' to attain union with God. Yet it would be wrong to read this in any Pelagian sense, as if the 'work' of contemplation is dependent on human effort alone. Nor is it God's work alone. Rather, the practice of contemplative prayer as depicted in *The Cloud* requires a partnership between God and the one praying, akin to Thomas Aquinas's notion of co-operative grace. For Thomas, 'God works, that we might desire: and when we desire, God cooperates with us that we might bring the desire to perfection.'[37] The fact that we desire God is the effect of God's operation (operative grace). Its source is God; we were created with the capacity to enter into relationship with God, reflected in the desire for God within us. God is the cause of this human longing, and God's grace moves us to pay attention to it. Once aware of the desire, one can choose to ignore or nourish it. As one who has chosen to nourish it, *The Cloud*'s addressee is told, 'Your part is to keep the windows and the door [of your soul] against the inroads of flies and enemies.' God is 'most willing' to help and 'only waiting for you' (2:119). This is co-operative grace: God working with the one who responds to God through the desire for God present deeply within the self. Furthermore, the whole practice of contemplation is itself a grace by which we are gradually reformed in likeness to God who 'fits himself exactly to our souls by adapting his Godhead to them; and our souls are fitted exactly to him by the worthiness of our creation after his image and likeness' (4:122). In other words there is a symbiosis between us and God. We were created with the capacity for union with God, who then fulfils that capacity with the offer of God's own self. The practice of apophatic contemplation is designed to enable the deepening of this union with God through grace.

The essence of *The Cloud*'s teaching on contemplation is simple in the extreme. Moved by the grace of the call to contemplation, one focuses one's desire upon God alone: 'Lift up your heart to God with a humble impulse of love; and have himself as your aim, not any of his goods. Take care that you avoid thinking of anything but himself so that there is nothing for your reason or your will to work on, except himself' (3:119–20). In order to facilitate this, the author counsels his advisee to place all creatures, including all images and thoughts even of God, 'beneath' him in 'a cloud of forgetting':

> Insofar as there is anything in your mind except God alone, in that far you are further from God (5:129) . . . The intense activity . . . of your understanding, which will always press upon you when you set yourself to this dark contemplation, must always be put down. If you do not put it down it will put you down. You will find that your

mind is occupied not with this darkness, but with a clear picture of something beneath God. (9:139)

Should thoughts come into the mind, as they inevitably will, the author counsels: 'Say [to such a thought] "You have no part to play . . . Go down again" [into the cloud of forgetting]. Tread it down quickly with an impulse of love, even though it seems to you to be very holy; even though it seems that it could help you to seek [God]' (7:132). It is important to be swift and relentless here, lest the thought 'increase its chattering more and more', distracting one completely from one's purpose (7:132), or worse, causing sinful 'pleasure or resentment' (10:142–3).

Instead, one is urged to focus upon the cloud of unknowing which exists between the self and God: 'You are to step above [any thought] stalwartly but lovingly, and with a devout, pleasing, impulsive love strive to pierce that darkness above you. You are to smite upon that thick cloud of unknowing with a sharp dart of longing love. Do not leave that work for anything that may happen' (6:131). This 'dart of love' is *The Cloud* author's favourite image for the activity proper to this type of prayer: 'The eye of your soul is opened on [the simple being of God] and fixed upon it, like the eye of the bowman upon the eye of the target that he is shooting at' (5:129). Only with such a steady gaze focused on the darkness, with much practice and perseverance, will the goal of union with God be attained. This steady gaze, this pure and simple gaze of love, is described, somewhat paradoxically, as 'blind' because of its lack of rational thought. It is not the abundance of sensual feeling but only the 'naked intent' of the will toward God. Representing the deepest desire of the soul, this 'naked intent' of the will seems to correspond to what Augustine meant by the *acies mentis*, the 'cutting edge' of the mind, the deepest point within the mind which 'overlaps with the eternal light it is in.'[38] It is here that God and the soul are one. Although *The Cloud* author does not advocate turning 'inward', as Hilton will, in order to seek God (cf. 68:251), the 'steady gaze' ascending to the cloud of unknowing seems to have its source deep within the self.

To facilitate the 'simple reaching out directly towards God', the author suggests using a mantra: 'If you like, you can have this reaching out, wrapped up and enfolded in a single word ... of one syllable rather than two; for the shorter it is the better it is in agreement with this exercise of the spirit. Such a one is the word "God" or the word "love." ... Fasten this word to your heart, so that whatever happens it will never go away' (7:133–4). Such a word focuses one's attention on the object of desire, God present in the cloud of unknowing, and acts as a twofold weapon: 'This word is to be your shield and your spear ... With this word you are to beat upon this cloud and this darkness above you. With this word you are to strike down every kind of thought under the cloud of forgetting' (7:134). Such a word can come to one's aid particularly in times of difficulty, when concentration is broken by distracting thoughts:

> Just as the little word "fire" suddenly beats upon and jars most effectively the ears of the bystanders, it is the same with the little word [used in prayer], whether spoken or thought ... It bursts upon the ears of almighty God much more than any long psalm mumbled away in an inarticulate fashion. And this is why it is written that a short prayer pierces heaven. (37:192–3)

The Cloud author explains union with God as simply a union of wills. However, he does suggest in one place that the intellect may be graced as a result: 'Perhaps it will be [God's] will to send out a ray of spiritual light ... and ... show you some of the divine secrets, of which one may not or cannot speak.' Furthermore, he admits, 'then you shall feel your affection all aflame with the fire of God's love, far more than I know how to tell you or may or wish to at this time' (26:174–5). This is as far as *The Cloud* author goes in describing the effects of mystical union, in great contrast to Rolle. In fact, he expresses disapproval of the sort of experiences Rolle endorsed: 'This blind impulse of love towards God for himself alone ... is more profitable ... than ... hearing all the mirth or the melody that is amongst those who are in bliss' (9:139–40). Again: 'All those who set themselves to be spiritual workers inwardly, and yet think that they ought either to hear, smell, see, taste or touch spiritual things, either within or outside themselves, surely they are deceived and are working wrongly' (70:255). He even goes farther, indulging in caricatures of 'false mystics' who look for such experiences in prayer:

> [They are] addicted to much strange behaviour, . . . staring like madmen do, . . . [their] eyes . . . set in their heads as though they were sheep suffering from the brain disease, and were near death's door. Some . . . hold their heads on one side as though a worm were in their ears. Some squeak instead of speaking normally . . . Some . . . gurgle and splutter in their throats (53:221–2) . . . They look up to the stars as though they would reach above the moon, and cock their ears as though they could hear angels sing out of heaven . . . Some of these the devil will delude in a remarkable manner. He will send down a sort of dew, which they think to be angels' food, which appears to come out of the air and falls softly and sweetly into their mouths. And so it is their habit to sit with their mouths open as though they were catching flies. (57:230–1)

Our author obviously has no time for religious posturing!

Rolle's writings, with their enthusiastic descriptions of the experiences of heat, sweetness and song, were popular throughout the fourteenth century. *The Cloud* author's reticence about describing experiences of mystical union is doubtless motivated by the fact that he knew people who sought such experiences for their own sake. He is aware of how easy it is for a beginner in contemplative prayer to be deceived and 'become the victim of spiritual illusion', which can happen in the following way:

> When young men or women who are beginners in the school of devotion hear this sorrow and this desire read or spoken about, how a man must lift up his heart to God and

desire without ceasing to experience the love of his God . . .
they understand these words not . . . spiritually, but car-
nally and physically, and they strive . . . to raise up the
heart in their breasts . . . They strain themselves and their
physical strength so roughly and so stupidly that within a
short time they fall victim to weariness . . . Or . . .
through . . . the way in which they play on their sensations
during the time of this false, animal and far from spiritual
exercise, it is likely that their hearts will be inflamed with
an unnatural fervour . . . or else there is created in their
imagination a false heat, the work of the devil . . . Yet, like
as not, they think that this is a fire of love produced and
kindled by the grace and goodness of the Holy Spirit. From
such illusions as these, and their ramifications, come great
mischief, great hypocrisy, great heresy and great error.
(45:205–7)

Instead *The Cloud* author intends to bring his addressee 'out of
the ignorant state of sensible feeling into the purity and depth
of spiritual feeling; and so finally to help you to fasten the
spiritual knot of burning love between you and your God in
spiritual oneness and union of wills' (47:210). In this effort, *The
Cloud* author is guided by Denis's notion that more sensual
experiences are farther away from God than those that are
more spiritual. The one who desires union with God, therefore,
'must live in the truth and depth of the spirit, far removed from
any bodily travesty of it . . . The more truly refined your spirit
is, the less it is contaminated by the sensible and the nearer
it is to God' (47:210–11).

Having said this, the author offers a caveat, as if afraid his
words will be interpreted as a negation of the body: 'God . . .
forbid that I should separate what he has joined together, the
body and the spirit; for it is God's will to be served both in body
and soul together' (48:212). Similarly, God sometimes rewards
contemplatives with bodily as well as spiritual blessings,
willing 'to set on fire the bodily senses of his devout servants
here in this life, and not once or twice but perhaps very often,

and according to his pleasure, with marvellous sweetness and consolation. Such consolations ... come from within, rising and springing up out of the abundance of spiritual gladness and of true devotion in the spirit' (48:212–13). However, *The Cloud* author counsels that such feelings are not to be confused with the act of contemplative prayer itself, nor should they be expected:

> No matter how pleasing they are, no matter how holy, we should have a sort of heedlessness [about them] ... If they come, welcome them; but do not depend too much on them because of your weakness; for to continue for long in those sweet experiences and tears is a great drain on your strength. It may be that you will be moved to love God simply for their sake. You will know that this is so if you grumble overmuch when they are withdrawn. If this is your experience, then your love is not yet either chaste or perfect. For when love is chaste and perfect, though it is content that the bodily senses be nourished and consoled through the presence of these experiences and tears, yet it does not grumble. It is well satisfied to do without them, if such be God's will. (50:216–17)

The author acknowledges that experiences among contemplatives differ: some enjoy felt consolation in prayer often, others rarely. One ought not consider such experience or its lack as an indication of greater or lesser holiness (50:217). Furthermore, it is wrong to judge one's own prayer by that of others, or vice versa. The graces of contemplation are gratuitous and received according to people's capacity and circumstances which may differ greatly. All of this is wise advice, as anyone knows who has attempted to develop a habit of prayer. Temptations to give up the practice when consolation is absent are common, as are the distractions incurred by wondering if one is 'doing it right'. Focusing the 'naked intent' of the will on God alone, rather than any feeling of consolation or expertise in prayer, is the essence of contemplation.

The other way *The Cloud* author talks about the effects of

prayer is by describing specific virtues that result from the grace of contemplation. Fundamental is the virtue of humility, modelled upon the example of Christ who desired 'to humble himself, so as to be on a level with you' (2:118–19). One practises humility by 'standing in desire . . . [wooing God] humbly in prayer', recognizing always one's utter need for God. It is important to remember this when efforts to be free of distraction are unsuccessful; one should then simply 'cower down under [the distraction] like a poor wretch and a coward overcome in battle', acknowledging humbly one's absolute need for God, who will then come 'to take you up, to cherish you and to dry your spiritual eyes, as the father does for the child' (32:181). The author distinguishes between imperfect and perfect humility. Humility in essence is truth: the understanding and awareness of self as one truly is. Imperfect humility sees oneself as wretched because it is rooted in sin, but perfect humility sees oneself only in contrast to the 'superabundant love and worthiness of God', at the sight of which 'all nature trembles.' It is simply the experience of creaturehood. Both types of humility are important. One cannot attain perfect humility without having imperfect humility first. Imperfect humility will disappear for the blessed in heaven, but perfect humility will remain (13–14:147–51).

The practical application of this discourse on humility for contemplative prayer is seen when the author counsels against perpetually wallowing in one's sin, under the mistaken notion that this is the meaning of humility. Reminders of past sins and temptations to new ones are the distractions most likely to hinder perseverance in prayer. They can engender discouragement over one's failure and weakness, focusing attention on oneself, rather than God. Instead, the examples of perfect humility to be kept in mind are Mary, the angels, and especially Christ, who called us 'to be as perfect by grace as he himself is by nature.' Growth in perfect humility may be achieved gradually by contemplatives on earth. Since they have renounced a life of sin and are growing in grace, they may well experience perfect humility from time to time, however rare and fleeting such experiences may be (13:151–3). Provided one has been absolved from sin through sacramental confession, one should 'choose rather to be humbled under the wonderful height and worthiness of God, which is perfect, rather than under [one's] own wretchedness, which is imperfect. That is to say, take care that you make the worthiness of God the object of your special contemplation, rather than your own wretchedness' (23:168). Like other distracting thoughts, memories of past sins should be placed firmly under the cloud of forgetting 'as soon as they arise' (31:180).

It is no surprise that the other virtue emphasized in *The Cloud* is charity, defined according to Jesus' rendering of the great commandment in the synoptic Gospels: 'the love of God for himself above all creatures, and the love of [others] equal to the love of yourself for God's sake' (24:169; cf. Mark 12:30–1). In the exercise of contemplation the first element of the defi- nition takes priority, since its essence 'is nothing else but a simple and direct reaching out to God for himself.' The one praying has no other desire than to love God for God's own sake. All else is forgotten: 'in this exercise, the perfect worker will not permit [an] awareness of the holiest creature God ever made to have any share' (24:170). Yet even though others are not in one's consciousness, the second element of the definition of charity, love for others, is perfectly fulfilled as well, for two reasons.

First, through the exercise of contemplation, in which one is not conscious of any particular persons, one is 'made so vir- tuous and so charitable ... that when he comes down to frequent the company of or to pray for his fellow-Christians, his will shall be directed as particularly towards his foe as towards his friend, towards the stranger as towards his kinsman ... All alike should be dear to him' (25:170–1). In other words, through contemplation, one's love is purified and one begins to love others with God's love for them.

The second reason why the command to love others is ful- filled through contemplation is rooted in theology: in the

doctrine of Christ's salvific death and in the Pauline image of
the Church as the Body of Christ (1 Corinthians 12):

> For as all . . . were lost in Adam, and as all . . . who bear
> witness to their desire of salvation by good works are saved
> and shall be by the power of Christ's passion alone, a soul
> whose affection is perfectly extended in this exercise and
> thus united to God in spirit . . . does all that in it lies . . . to
> make all . . . as perfect in this work as it is itself. For just as
> when a limb of our body feels sore, all the other limbs are
> in pain and ill-affected on that account, or when one limb
> is in good health, all the rest are likewise in good health; so
> it is, spiritually, with all the limbs of holy church . . . And
> whoever desires to be a perfect disciple of our Lord is called
> upon to lift up his spirit in this spiritual exercise for the
> salvation of all his natural brothers and sisters, as our
> Lord lifted up his body on the cross. (25:171–2)

The Cloud author understands the act of contemplation as participating somehow in Christ's passion, as sharing in Christ's
love for others through the giving of oneself to God on their
behalf. When the contemplative spends time with God, focusing
solely upon God, all others are somehow present before God
with the one praying, and benefit from that prayer, because of
the unity of the Body of Christ. In a sense, this theology makes
contemplative prayer an extension of the meaning of eucharist.
This passage in particular reveals clearly the author's firm
grounding in the Christian scriptural and theological tradition
and in the communal life of the Church.

4. THE MASTER: WALTER HILTON

Reforming in faith is common to all chosen souls, though they are only in the lowest degree of charity; but reforming in feeling pertains especially to such souls as can come to the state of perfection – and that cannot be had suddenly: but a soul can come to it after great abundance of grace and great spiritual labor, and that is when [one] is first healed of . . . spiritual sickness, when all bitter passions, carnal pleasures and other old feelings are burnt out of the heart with the fire of desire, and new gracious feelings are brought in, with burning love and spiritual light: then a soul draws near to perfection and to reforming in feeling . . . But a soul cannot suddenly jump from the lowest to the highest, any more than someone wanting to climb a high ladder and setting [a] foot upon the lowest rung can next fly up to the highest. [One] needs to go gradually, one [step] after another, until [one] can come to the top. It is just the same spiritually. Nobody is suddenly made perfect in grace, but through long exercise and skilled working may come to it when a wretched soul is taught and helped by [God] in whom lies all grace.

The Scale of Perfection 2:17[1]

The title of Walter Hilton's masterpiece *The Scale of Perfection* (sometimes translated *The Ladder* or *The Stairway of Perfection*) did not originate with Hilton himself, though it is found in about half of the manuscripts. It is drawn from the image of the ladder in the above quotation, which is an apt symbol for what Hilton intends in both books of *The Scale*: to present the progress of the Christian life step by step, systematically, in close conjunction with the chief doctrines of the Christian faith. Phyllis Hodgson suggests he is 'first and foremost a teacher, restrained and methodical, guided by reason, orthodoxy and tradition', yet his presentation of doctrine is illustrated with concrete images that 'adorn while elucidating' his themes.[2] His subject matter is a clear, no-frills presentation of Christian life and doctrine, less idiosyncratic than Rolle's works and less esoteric than those of *The Cloud* author. As such, Hilton's teaching applies to all the baptized, and not merely to a small minority of people in the vowed or anchoritic life. Hilton is a bit more theologically conservative than either Rolle or *The Cloud* author, and more obviously devoted to an explicitly orthodox spirituality, but this does not prevent him from suggesting creative innovations where they seem appropriate.

HILTON'S LIFE AND WRITINGS

The one certain fact about Walter Hilton is that he died an Augustinian canon at the priory of Thurgarton (between Nottingham and Newark) on 23/24 March 1395/6. The rest of his life story is speculation based upon meagre historical evidence.[3] He was probably born in the early 1340s, no later than 1343. It is virtually certain that he studied at Cambridge, possibly arriving there around 1357. He may have studied civil law and practised as a lawyer for a time; he also studied theology, again at Cambridge, and was ordained a priest, possibly by 1371. Afterwards, he continued his studies, becoming an inceptor in canon law around 1381/2.[4] The title 'Master', indicating an advanced university degree, precedes his name on some manuscripts. Thus, Hilton likely had the most extensive formal education of all the English mystics. In his earliest extant work (*De imagine peccati*), Hilton remarks that he was living as a solitary, but was dissatisfied with the life, wishing to be of more practical service to God and Church. The 'mixed life' of the Augustinian canons was better suited to his character. After much exploration and testing of various lifestyles, Hilton entered Thurgarton Priory, probably by 1386.

Besides *The Scale of Perfection*, Hilton authored other works, which provide a window into his character. His earliest, *De imagine peccati* (*On the Image of Sin*) is a short tract on the effects of original sin in epistolary form written to a solitary. A second Latin letter, *De utilitate et prerogativis religionis* (*On the Usefulness and Prerogatives of Religion*), is a defence of communal religious life written to Adam Horsley, a public official considering monastic life, who eventually entered the Beauvale Charterhouse in 1386. In the letter, Hilton claims that he himself is contemplating religious life. He wrote two other letters in a similar vein, counselling people about their state of life. *Mixed Life* is written to a layman with a family and heavy social responsibilities. Hilton advises him not to try to live like a monk, but to adopt a style of spirituality more conducive to his circumstances. A final Latin letter, *Epistola ad quemdam secula renuntiare volentem* (*Letter to Someone Wanting to Renounce the World*) is addressed to a lawyer who has experienced a conversion from a worldly and self-centred lifestyle. Hilton dissuades him from considering religious life, judging it unsuited to his temperament, but encourages him in his efforts to reform his living. These letters provide insight into the breadth of Hilton's acquaintances, indicating his renown as a spiritual guide, not only for religious, but for layfolk as well. He had more extensive experience with secular activity in the everyday world than either Rolle or *The Cloud* author, which helps explain why his presentation of Christian holiness differs somewhat from theirs.

Three other works by Hilton can be classified as cautions against certain religious tendencies and practices prevalent in his day. *Conclusiones de imaginibus* (*Conclusions concerning Images*) is a defence of the veneration of images in opposition to the Lollards. It is conceivable that Hilton participated in the Church's initial action against Wyclif as one of a group of clerks retained by Thomas Arundel, then Bishop of Ely, to prepare a response to Wyclif's teachings. Later, when his prior at Thurgarton was given authority to examine suspected Lollards, Hilton's legal expertise may have been tapped for this endeavour. A second work, *Epistole de lectione, intentione, oratione, meditatione, etc.* (*On Reading, Intention, Prayer, Meditation, etc.*), defends the common prayer of the Church, particularly the divine office and the practice of *lectio divina*, against any 'liberty of spirit' which would set such practices aside for the sake of 'higher' illumination. This was most likely directed against the Free Spirit controversy, but it is not inconceivable that Hilton also had a work like *The Cloud* in mind. Finally, *On Angels' Song* is a critique of enthusiastic, sensually-oriented prayer as practised by followers of Richard Rolle. Like *The Cloud* author, Hilton expresses concern that over-enthusiastic beginners in prayer might leave discursive meditation aside too soon, mistaking sensual religious feeling for true contemplation.

Two translations have been attributed to Hilton: the English version of *Eight Chapters on Perfection*, written by Luis de Fontibus, a Spanish Franciscan, and James of Milan's *Stimulus amoris*, entitled in English *The Pricking* (or *The Goad*) *of Love*. Finally, an English commentary on Psalm 90, *Qui habitat*, should almost certainly be attributed to Hilton.

The Scale of Perfection is really two books in one, written on related topics at different times, each of which circulated independently of the other. Comparison between the two reveals a change in Hilton's thinking about the nature and scope of contemplation. In *Scale* 1, addressed to an anchoress, Hilton follows tradition by equating action and contemplation with specific states of life, in a way similar to Rolle and *The Cloud* (cf. 1:2–3, 78–9). But in *Scale* 2 he presents contemplation as the destiny of all the baptized:[5] 'There can be many different ways and diverse practices leading different souls to contemplation ... according to people's various dispositions and the different states they are in, such as seculars and those in religious orders' (2:7, 245). Thus every baptized person

should desire always to feel the lively inspiration of grace caused by the spiritual presence of Jesus in our soul, if we could, and to have him always with reverence in our sight; and always to feel the sweetness of his love by a wonderful homeliness of his presence . . . See, this feeling is for us to desire since every rational soul should long with all its powers to draw near to Jesus and to become one with him through the feeling of his gracious invisible presence. (2:41, 287–8)

What follows here examines each book of *The Scale* in turn, the discussion of Book 1 focusing on the Augustinian tradition which influenced Hilton, and that of Book 2 on the creative refinements Hilton made to that tradition.

SCALE 1: AUGUSTINE'S LEGACY

Augustine of Hippo (354–430) is among the most attractive and stimulating theological geniuses in Christian history. His influence upon theology has been massive, so much so that all medieval theology in the West has been called a mere footnote to Augustine.[6] All of the authors we have described so far, Rolle, *The Cloud* author, and those they used as sources (with the exception of Denis) were heavily influenced by Augustine. With Hilton, the influence of Augustine appears more clearly and directly, because Hilton organizes his work around specific and obvious Augustinian themes.[7]

Both books of *The Scale* focus on the *imago Dei* tradition, the notion that the human soul was created in the image and likeness of God (Genesis 1:26–7). This image was subsequently defaced by sin, but through Christ the grace necessary for its restoration has become available. In the West, this theme was creatively modified by Augustine, who described the soul more precisely as created in the image of the Trinity.[8] Hilton's indebtedness to Augustine is evident in the following passage:

The soul . . . is a life made of three powers – memory, reason and will – in the image and likeness of the blessed Trinity: whole, perfect and righteous. The memory has the

> likeness of the Father, inasmuch as it was made strong and
> steadfast by the Father's omnipotence, to hold him without
> forgetting, distraction, or hindrance from any creature.
> The reason was made clear and bright, without error or
> darkness ... and so it has the likeness of the Son, who is
> infinite wisdom. And the love and the will were made pure,
> burning towards God without animal pleasure in the flesh
> or in any creature, by the supreme goodness; and it has
> the likeness of the Holy Spirit, who is blessed love. So [the]
> soul, which may be called a created trinity, was filled with
> memory, sight and love by the uncreated blessed Trinity.
> (1:43, 113–14)[9]

Augustine maintained that this image of God in the soul's
faculties of memory, understanding and will was ineradicable,
remaining constant in spite of the tragedy of sin. Later writers,
like Hugh of St Victor, Bonaventure and Bernard, distin-
guished between the image and likeness mentioned in Genesis.
The image, understood as mimetic, remains in the soul in spite
of sin, simply representing the pattern of the Trinity, as a map
represents a geographical terrain. 'Likeness' means much
more, being a participation in the life of the Trinity, which was
lost to the soul through sin.[10] Hilton follows the later writers,
understanding the Christian life as a gradual 'reforming' of
this lost likeness to God in the soul.

Furthermore, for Hilton, as a result of sin the image of the
Trinity has become corrupted, participating in sin rather than
in God, appearing ironically as an *imago peccati* (image of sin),
'a foul, dark, wretched trinity', which Hilton describes thus:

> As the memory was at one time stable in God, so now it has
> forgotten [God] and looks for its rest in created things ...
> It is just the same with the reason [which is ignorant of
> God] and likewise the love, which was pure in spiritual
> savor and sweetness; now it is turned into a foul bestial
> pleasure and delight in [itself] and created things, and
> carnal savors, both through the senses (as in gluttony
> and lechery), and by imagination (as in pride, vainglory

and covetousness) . . . This puts out the love of God from the heart, in feeling and spiritual savor, so that it cannot come in. (1:43, 114)

Such is the legacy of original sin, exacerbated by 'all the other wretchedness and sins . . . voluntarily added to it' (1:43, 114).

Hilton also follows Augustine in teaching that knowledge of God is linked to true knowledge of oneself. Because the image of God, however obscured by sin, remains in the soul, the search for God involves a journey within.[11] This theme is introduced on the very first page of *The Scale*: 'Any man or woman is wretched who neglects all the inward keeping of the self in order to fashion only an outward form and semblance of holiness' (1:1, 77). Later Hilton advises, 'Enter into your own soul by meditation in order to know what it is, and by the knowledge of it to come to the spiritual knowledge of God. For as St. Augustine says: "By the knowledge of myself I shall get the knowledge of God" ' (1:40, 110).[12] Hilton calls this inward journey 'a plain highway to contemplation', as a result of which one discovers the desire 'to recover that dignity and honor' which was lost through sin (1:42, 112). This desire within, which is essentially the desire for God, figures prominently in Augustine's theology, evident, for example, in the prayer to God articulated at the beginning of his most famous work, the *Confessions*: 'You have made us for yourself, and our heart is restless until it rests in you.'[13]

Another aspect of the *imago Dei* tradition involves Christ. Humans are said to be created *in* the image of God; they are not themselves, strictly speaking, *the* image of God. That designation is reserved to the second person of the Trinity, who is God's self-expression, God's Word, God's Wisdom, God's Image, in and through whom humans were created. This Word made flesh in Jesus becomes, for Hilton, the focus of the soul's desire to recover its own lost likeness to God. Thus, the desire which arises as a result of the journey within is summed up in the desire for Jesus:

I shall speak one word for all that you shall seek, desire

and find, for in that word is all that you have lost. This
word is Jesus ... I mean Jesus, all goodness, infinite
wisdom, love and sweetness, your joy, your worship and
your everlasting bliss, your God, your Lord and your
salvation ... Lift up the desire of your heart to Jesus –
even though you are blind and can see nothing of him – and
say that he it is whom you have lost, him you want to have,
and nothing but him: no other joy, no other bliss, in heaven
or on earth, but him ... Always be longing for Jesus more
and more, to find him better ... However much you know
or feel of him here in this life, he is still above it. And
therefore if you want to find him fully as he is in the bliss of
loving, never cease from spiritual desire as long as you live.
(1:46, 119)

Where does one seek Jesus? Like the woman searching for her
lost coin (Luke 15:8–10), the seeker must look for Jesus within
one's own house, within the self, where Jesus lies hidden like
the treasure in the field (Matthew 13:44) or where Jesus sleeps
as he once did in the ship at sea (Matthew 8:23–7). The 'lantern'
used to aid one's search is reason, fuelled by the light of God's
word, provided it is lifted above the detritus of sin in the soul:

There is no one who lights a lamp in order to set it under a
bushel, but on a candlestick [Matthew 5:15]. That is to say,
the reason shall not be covered up with worldly thoughts
and business, or with vain thoughts and carnal affections,
but always lifted as high as you can ... By this lantern you
can find Jesus. (1:48, 121)[14]

Because Jesus is obscured by 'the mess and filth and small
specks of dust in your house, all the carnal loves and fears in
your soul', like the woman of the Gospel, the seeker must sweep
the house: 'You shall turn all such sins out of your heart, and
sweep your soul clean with the broom of the fear of God,
and wash it with the water of your eyes; and so you will find
this coin Jesus. He is the coin, he is the penny, and he is your
heritage.' This work of housecleaning is not easy, 'not the work

of one hour, or one day, but of many days and years, with great sweat and toil of the body and labor of the soul' (1:48, 121). The difficulty of the task is spelled out in the rest of Book 1 of *The Scale* (chapters 52–89), describing the 'ground of sin' present in the soul. Hilton does not mean actual sin as such, but the disordered desires or tendencies toward sin which remain as the legacy of original sin. Here Hilton is clearly indebted to the instructional manuals on sin prevalent in the fourteenth century. He describes the seven deadly sins in great detail along with incentives to acquire their opposite virtues. As in *The Cloud,* the virtues of humility and charity take precedence.

It is frequently noted that Book 1 of *The Scale* is concerned mostly with the earlier stages of the journey toward holiness, with the purgative and illuminative ways predominating. However, Hilton is less concerned with absolute distinctions about stages of spiritual progress than many spiritual writers before him. He is more interested in describing the continuity of growth in the life of grace, the goal of which is union with God. His description of contemplation, even in *Scale* 1, is broader than that of *The Cloud* author, or even of Rolle.

For Hilton there are three 'parts' to contemplation. The first part involves the rational powers of the soul: 'the knowledge of God and the things of the spirit, acquired by reason, by [human] teaching ... and by the study of holy scripture.' A scholar himself, Hilton values the role theology can play in bringing one to contemplative prayer: 'this part belongs especially to some learned men and great scholars who by long study and labor in holy scripture come to this knowledge.' Although he warns that such knowledge can encourage pride or vainglory, it can also 'strongly dispose' one to prayer, and be a step to the fullness of contemplation (1:4, 79–80).

The second part of contemplation concerns the affective powers of the soul, which, under the influence of grace, experience 'a fervor of love and spiritual sweetness in the remembrance of [Christ's] passion' or 'trust in the goodness and mercy of God for the forgiveness of sins, and for his great gifts of grace', or a lessening of the desire for 'earthly things'. The 'sweet tears, burning desires and still mournings' in this stage, typical of the experience of compunction, 'scour and cleanse the heart from all the filth of sin and make it melt into a wonderful sweetness of Jesus Christ – obedient, supple and ready to fulfill all God's will' (1:5, 80).[15]

Once one has been 'cleansed from all sins and reformed to the image of Jesus by completeness of virtue', one may well enjoy the third part of contemplation, which involves both the rational and affective powers of the soul. Hilton avoids the tendency of *The Cloud* to deny the intellect a role in the experience of union with God. One is 'illumined by the grace of the Holy Spirit to see intellectually the Truth, which is God, and also spiritual things, with a soft, sweet burning love for [God] – so perfectly that by the rapture of this love the soul is for the time united and conformed to the image of the Trinity.' In this union 'God and the soul are not two, but both are one', enjoying a 'marriage . . . which shall never be broken' (1:8, 82). The marriage may be unbroken, but human 'feeling' of the rapture of this union is sporadic and fleeting. It is a foretaste of the union one will enjoy with God in heaven; only the beginning of it can be experienced in this life, its fullness being reserved for eternity.

SCALE 2: HILTON'S REFINEMENT OF AUGUSTINE

Book 2 of *The Scale* begins with a review of the *imago Dei* theme described in Book 1, followed by a summary of Anselm's argument for the atonement. After this theological introduction, Hilton presents his schema for the 'reforming' of the likeness to God which is the project of the baptismal life of grace. The fullness of this reforming is reserved to the blessed in heaven, but a partial reforming can happen in this life. It is of two kinds: reforming in faith and reforming in feeling. One source for the distinction between them is the Isaian passage: 'Unless you first believe, you cannot understand' (Isaiah 7:9). As Hilton explains, 'Faith goes before, and understanding

comes after; and that understanding I call the sight of God.'
This is experienced in contemplation, the goal of the baptismal
life of grace (2:11, 210). He then contrasts the two:

> The first, which is reforming in faith alone, is sufficient for
> salvation; the second is worthy of surpassing reward in the
> bliss of heaven. The first may be gained easily and in a
> short time; the second not so, but through length of time
> and great spiritual labor. The first can be had together
> with the feeling of the image of sin, for though [one]
> feels . . . stirrings of sin and fleshly desires . . . [one] may be
> reformed in faith to the likeness of God. But the second
> reforming drives out the enjoyment and feeling of fleshly
> stirrings and worldly desires and allows no such spots to
> remain in this image . . . By the first reforming the image
> of sin is not destroyed, but it is left as if all whole in feeling;
> but the second reforming destroys the old feelings of this
> image of sin and brings into the soul new gracious feelings
> through the working of the Holy Spirit. The first is good;
> the second is better, but the third, which is in the bliss of
> heaven, is best of all. (2:5, 199–200)

Hilton emphasizes that reform in faith is made possible first
through baptism, and then continually through the sacrament
of penance. But one reformed only in faith will be continually
bothered by the 'carnal stirrings of the image of sin' which are
at battle with the longing for God. A further reform, a reform in
feeling, is needed to silence sinful urges within the self and
replace them solely with the desire for God and the things of
God.

Here Hilton draws upon yet another Augustinian theme:
that of the divided will and the consequent need for grace.
Augustine taught that sin left the will in a weakened state.
Divided within itself, drawn toward both good and evil, it
cannot desire the good thoroughly enough to withstand the
attraction of evil. Human free will or freedom of choice (*libero
arbitrio*) is not enough; something more is needed to heal the
will from within, making it whole, strengthening its desire for

God so completely that one becomes free to act on that desire. Augustine called this *libertas*, the liberating grace that gives humans the freedom to desire what God desires, to love what God loves, to delight in what God delights in, so strongly that the power of the attraction to evil is overcome and one is enabled to do good.[16] Hilton's reform in feeling is his own creative adaptation of this Augustinian teaching.

Like Augustine, Hilton describes the divided will within the self, by paraphrasing Paul:

> I have found two laws in myself: one law in my soul within, and another . . . fighting with it, that often leads me like a wretched prisoner to the law of sin. By these two laws in a soul I understand this double image: by the law of the spirit I understand the reason of the soul when it is reformed to the image of God; by the law of the flesh I understand the sensuality, which I call the image of sin . . . In my soul, that is, in my will and in my reason, I serve the law of God; but in my flesh, that is, in my carnal appetite, I serve the law of sin . . . I do not perform the good I would like to do, that is, I would like to feel no carnal stirring, and that I do not; but I do the evil that I hate, that is, the sinful stirrings of my flesh. I hate them and yet I feel them. (2:11, 208–9)[17]

Hilton is using the distinction Paul draws between 'spirit' and 'flesh', which he probably understands in the Pauline sense. It would be a mistake to interpret these terms as referring to soul and body as such. Rather, 'spirit' designates the human being as related to God under the influence of grace, while 'flesh' designates the human being apart from God and prone to the influence of sin. In the tradition following Augustine, 'flesh' became 'concupiscence', a reluctance or languor toward the things of God with a corresponding attraction toward evil. It is experienced primarily in the senses, making one unwilling or unable to pursue goodness.[18] Certain phrases used by Hilton, like 'carnal appetite' or 'sinful stirrings of the flesh' should not be read as a denigration of the body and its impulses as such, but as referring to that concupiscence experienced in the body as an effect of sin. Similarly, phrases which encourage a withdrawal from 'the world' are not meant to deny the fundamental goodness of creation, but warn against the disordered desire to seek fulfilment in earthly things rather than in God.

For Hilton, being reformed in faith through baptism is the first step toward the elimination of those 'carnal stirrings' that keep one from the fullness of grace. However, in *Scale* 2 he is more concerned with the various steps of the 'ladder' one must climb to move from mere reform in faith to reform in feeling. He organizes these steps according to his interpretation of another Pauline passage: 'These that God knew before, that were to be made to conform to the image of his Son: these he called; these he corrected; these he magnified; and these he glorified.'[19] The first step is a 'calling from worldly vanity', during which one feels much consolation, 'for at the beginning of conversion a person who is disposed to abundant grace is so vitally and perceptibly inspired, and often feels such great sweetness of devotion, with so many tears in compunction, that he sometimes feels as if he were half in heaven.' By contrast, the second step, the 'time of correcting' is wearisome: one is hindered from reaching one's desire for Jesus and is 'vexed by various temptations . . . until all the rust of impurity can be burnt out.' Often one feels 'forsaken by God . . . except for a little secret trust . . . in the goodness of God.' When one is sufficiently 'mortified' one advances to the next step, the time of 'magnifying . . . when the soul is partly reformed in feeling, and receives the gift of perfection and the grace of contemplation, and that is a time of great rest.' Finally comes the fourth step, the time of 'glorifying . . . when the soul shall be fully reformed in the bliss of heaven, . . . [raised] to equality with the Cherubim and Seraphim' (2:28, 248–9).

A second image Hilton uses to describe the process of reform in feeling is that of pilgrimage to Jerusalem, a favourite devotional practice in the fourteenth century. The word 'Jerusalem' signifies 'sight of peace', the goal of the Christian life: 'contemplation in perfect love of God . . . nothing other than a

sight of Jesus, who is true peace' (2:21, 227). This is that perfect
'reform in feeling' which will be enjoyed in heaven, but also
experienced partially in this life through the gift of contemplation. Hilton develops his pilgrimage analogy thus:

> The beginning of the highway along which you shall go is
> reforming in faith, grounded humbly in the faith and in the
> laws of holy church . . . If you want to speed on your travels
> and make a good journey each day, you should hold these
> two things often in your mind – humility and love. That is:
> *I am nothing; I have nothing; I desire only one thing.* You
> shall have the meaning of these words continually in your
> intention . . . Humility says, I am nothing; I have nothing.
> Love says, I desire only one thing, and that is Jesus. (2:21,
> 228)

Hilton repeats over and over this twin desire – to have nothing
and to seek Jesus – seeming to suggest that it function as a
kind of mantra in one's prayer. He shifts from his pilgrimage
analogy to a musical one to describe the virtues of humility and
love:

> These two strings, well-fastened with mindfulness of
> Jesus, make good harmony on the harp of the soul when
> they are skillfully touched with the finger of reason. For
> the lower you strike upon one, the higher sounds the other;
> the less you feel that you are or that you have of yourself
> through humility, the more you long to have of Jesus in the
> desire of love. (2:21, 228)

Hilton provides a definition of humility similar to *The Cloud*'s
'perfect humility': what 'the soul feels through grace in seeing
and considering the infinite being and wonderful goodness of
Jesus, . . . for in comparison with Jesus who is in truth All, you
are but nothing' (2:21, 228).

Just as a pilgrim to Jerusalem must leave everything behind
and 'travel light', so Hilton advises, 'Make yourself naked of all
that you have – both good works and bad – and throw them
all behind you; and thus become so poor in your own feeling

that there can be no deed of your own that you want to lean upon for rest, ... always seeking the spiritual presence of Jesus.' Just as a traveller needs a clear destination, so for the contemplative: 'You shall set in your heart, wholly and fully, your will to have nothing but the love of Jesus and the spiritual sight of him' (2:21, 229). Something like *The Cloud*'s 'naked intent of the will' is referred to here, but with an entirely different flavour. One is similarly urged to single-heartedness, putting everything aside save the desire for God, but here the focus is not the dark cloud of unknowing, but the person of Jesus, whom the one praying hopes to see 'spiritually' more and more.

Just as the pilgrim can expect to encounter hardships and delays on the journey, so the person intent on spiritual growth can expect to fight 'carnal desires and vain fears' which 'hinder [one's] desire for the love of God.' The antidote is simply to keep focused on Jesus. There is no need to backtrack over past sins, brooding over one's unworthiness. Instead Hilton counsels, 'Trust firmly that you are on the road ... Keep up your desire, and say nothing else but that you want to have Jesus and to be in Jerusalem ... Stop thinking of that distress and go forth to your work' (2:22, 230–2). For to desire Jesus is to have him: 'When you feel your thought taken up with desire for Jesus by the touching of his grace, ... think then that you have Jesus, for he it is that you desire.' With such a guide as Jesus, one will be perfectly safe: 'Behold him well, for he goes before you ... Trust him and follow him wheresoever he goes, for he shall lead you in the right way to Jerusalem: that is, the sight of peace in contemplation' (2:24, 234).

This journey to Jerusalem takes place within, and Hilton reiterates the theme from *Scale* 1 that the way to knowledge of God is through knowing oneself:

> A soul that wants to have knowledge of spiritual things needs first to have knowledge of itself ... For your soul is only a mirror in which you shall see God spiritually. Therefore, you shall first find your mirror and keep it bright and clean from fleshly filth and worldly vanity, and

> hold it well up from the earth so that you can see it, and in
> it likewise our Lord. For this is the end for which all chosen
> souls labor in this life. (2:30, 252–3)

Hilton makes it perfectly clear that this journey is for all the
baptized, no matter what their state of life, and that it may be
reached through different routes:

> Whatever work it is that you should do, in body or in spirit,
> according to the degree and state in which you stand, if it
> helps this grace-given desire that you have to love
> Jesus, . . . that is the work I consider the best, whether it
> be prayer, meditation, reading or working; and as long as
> that task most strengthens your heart and your will for the
> love of Jesus . . . it is good to use it. (2:21, 229)

A third image Hilton uses to describe the process of the
reform in feeling is that of two days separated by a night. He
begins with a paraphrase of Isaiah 26:8–9: 'Lord Jesus, the
remembrance of you is impressed on the desire of my soul, for
my soul has desired you in the night, and my spirit has longed
for you in all my thoughts' (2:24, 234). Hilton explains this
night as a 'night of the spirit' separating two lights, just as the
actual night separates day from day. In the process of reform in
feeling, it is necessary to pass by means of this night from the
'false light' of a corrupted 'love of this world', which is the legacy
of sin, to the 'true light' which is 'the perfect love of Jesus
felt . . . through grace' (2:24, 234). He explains,

> This night is nothing but a separation and withdrawal of
> the thought of the soul from earthly things, by great desire
> and yearning to love, see and feel Jesus and the things of
> the spirit . . . This is a good night and a luminous darkness,
> for it is a shutting out of the false love of this world, and it
> is a drawing near to the true day. (2:24, 235)

The phrase 'luminous darkness' comes from Denis, signifying
for him the excess of God's light that blinds the intellect,[20] but
Hilton means something very different by it. For him it

describes a condition within humanity encountered in the search for God within the self.[21] When the familiar 'carnal desires' are deadened, one experiences a 'night' or emptiness within until the true light of Christ dawns.

In the beginning of the reform in feeling, this night is painful, because efforts to focus one's desire on God alone are thwarted by the impulse to return to familiar 'carnal affections and earthly things'. Hilton advises having patience with oneself: 'Do not be heavyhearted and do not strive too hard ... Draw your desire and the regard of your spirit toward Jesus.' Gradually, the night becomes comforting, the means through which 'a soul can through grace be gathered into itself and stay still in itself, freely and wholly.' One 'thinks of no earthly thing in a way that can attach it. This is a rich nothing, ... a great ease for the soul that desires the love of Jesus.' One eventually realizes that this night 'is not all dark and negative ... since Jesus, who is both love and light, is in this darkness.' The night is an in-between time where one is neither in the false light of the world nor in the true light of union with Jesus, a time of waiting for 'that blessed love of God which [one] desires' (2:24, 236–7).

Hilton uses another quotation from Isaiah to encourage perseverance in this darkness: 'For the dwellers in the land of the shadow of death, light has arisen [Isaiah 9:2]. That is, the light of grace rose and shall rise for those that know how to stay in ... this darkness that is like death.' Just as death kills all bodily feelings, so one's deep desire for Jesus uncovered in this darkness kills all sinful feelings and urges, and leads one closer to Jerusalem. Therefore, Hilton counsels,

> Apply your heart fully to the stirring of grace, grow used to staying in this darkness, and try often to feel at home in it. It will soon be made restful to you, and the true light of spiritual knowledge shall arise for you: not all at once, but secretly and little by little ... You are fast drawing near to Jerusalem. You are not there yet, but before you come to it you will be able to see it from afar, by the small sudden

gleams that shine through little crannies from that city.
(2:25, 238)

It is impossible to reconstruct in these few pages all the specific
advice Hilton gives about how to behave in this sort of prayer.
Suffice it to say it is wise and practical, full of lovely meditations drawn from particular scriptural passages such as
those I have cited as examples above.

If one perseveres through this night, God eventually 'opens
the inner eyes of the soul, to see him and know him; not all at
once, but little by little at different times.' This 'sight' of God is
thus a kind of knowing, 'strengthened and illuminated by the
gift of the Holy Spirit, with a wonderful reverence and a secret
burning love, and with spiritual savor and heavenly delight'
(2:32, 259). As a consequence, one's whole life begins to be
directed by this spiritual sight and knowledge of God. One is
reformed in likeness to Jesus who 'brings into the soul the
fullness of virtues', which are no longer difficult to practise.
'The virtues of humility and patience, sobriety and constancy,
chastity and purity, kindness toward [one's] fellow
Christians ... are now turned into softness and pleasure and
wonderful lightness of heart' (2:36, 270–1).

Hilton hesitates to say more about the 'opening of the spiritual eye', claiming humbly that it is beyond his experience (note
the contrast to Rolle). He lists a host of descriptive phrases
'from various men in holy writing' to characterize it: 'purity
of spirit and spiritual rest, inward stillness and peace of
conscience, highness of thought and solitude of soul, a lively
feeling of grace and secrecy of heart, the waking sleep of the
spouse and tasting of heavenly savor, burning in love and
shining in light, entrance to contemplation and reforming in
feeling' (2:40, 280–1).[22]

One of the effects of the opening of the spiritual eye is a
growth in the ability to understand Scripture. 'Grace puts vocal
prayer to silence and stirs the soul to see and feel Jesus in
another way: ... in holy scripture. For Jesus, who is all truth, is
hidden and concealed there ... Jesus is the well of wisdom, and

by a little pouring of his wisdom into a pure soul he makes the
soul wise enough to understand all holy scripture' (2:43, 293)
just as he did for the two disciples on the road to Emmaus
(Luke 24:45). There follows a substantial lesson on how to read,
interpret and pray with Scripture. Like Rolle, Hilton exhibits
the desire that Scripture be more readily accessible to his
readers. Both books of *The Scale* are peppered with scriptural
citations, inserted into the text first in Latin, followed by an
English translation or paraphrase. It is evident that Hilton's
opposition to Lollardy did not cause him to disavow the importance of adequate access to Scripture in the vernacular for those
who could not read Latin. Furthermore, Hilton considers a
greater facility to understand Scripture one of the fruits of
contemplation, rather than merely a step leading up to it, as in
The Cloud.

The thoroughgoing nature of Hilton's Christocentrism is
striking, and *The Scale* contains some of the loveliest, most
heartfelt meditations on Jesus to be found in all devotional
literature. This makes *The Scale* very different in tone from
The Cloud, which barely mentions Jesus, and even from Rolle's
writings, which sometimes relegate Christocentric meditation
to the lower levels of spiritual progress, and are generally more
interested in describing the graces of contemplation than
focusing upon Christ as such.[23] For Hilton, the whole journey
toward perfection is centred on Christ, however one's prayer
might change as one advances in the life of contemplation. In a
passage which exhibits some dependence on Bernard's stages
of love, Hilton describes three kinds of love: 'The first comes
through faith alone, without the grace of imagination or spiritual knowledge of God.' Here one simply believes what one has
learned about Jesus through church teaching. The second type
of love is 'what a soul feels through faith and the imagination of
Jesus in his humanity . . . when the imagination is stirred by
grace', and Jesus is approached through the feelings of devotion
or compunction. Here belongs the practice of affective meditation on the life and passion of Christ. Hilton stresses that this
type of love is good, and indeed essential for a time. The third

type of love 'is what the soul feels through spiritual sight of the divine nature in the manhood' of Jesus, which 'is more honorable, more spiritual and more deserving of reward than the consideration of the manhood alone' (2:30, 253–4).

In the process of spiritual growth, one may be called to leave aside imaginative meditations on Christ's humanity, along with their felt consolations, for a different type of prayer. Hilton uses the Gospel story of Christ's appearance to Mary Magdalene to make his point:

> This was our Lord's teaching to Mary Magdalene . . . when he spoke thus, *Noli me tangere* . . . Do not touch me [John 20:17]; . . . that is to say, Mary Magdalene ardently loved our Lord Jesus before the time of his passion, but her love was much in the body, little in the spirit . . . She allowed all her affection and all her thought to go to him as he was, in the form of man . . . But afterward, when he had risen from death and appeared to her, she would have honored him with the same kind of love as she did before, and then our Lord forbade her, saying thus . . . Do not set the rest or the love of your heart upon that human form . . . to rest in it . . . [But] make me a God in your heart and in your love, and worship me in your understanding as Jesus, God in man – supreme truth, supreme goodness and blessed life. (2:30, 255–6)[24]

Hilton is suggesting that, when one passes through the 'night' into higher contemplation, one's prayer becomes less a meditation on the life of Jesus or even prayer *to* Jesus, but is simply the quiet realization of Christ's divine presence within oneself. This presence fills one with wisdom to understand in some dim way the things of God and to live as Jesus lived.

In one of the final chapters of *The Scale* Hilton speaks of 'the hidden voice of Jesus sounding in a soul' and of certain 'illuminations' which can be called the 'sayings of Jesus'. Once the spiritual eye of the soul is opened 'Jesus shows more, leads the soul further inward, and begins to speak more familiarly and more lovingly to a soul.' Hilton describes such experience:

When [this voice] sounds in a soul it is so strong sometimes that the soul at once lays aside all that there is – praying, speaking, reading or meditation ... and every kind of bodily work – and listens to it fully, hearing and perceiving the sweet sound of this spiritual voice in rest and in love, as if ravished from the awareness of all earthly things. And then in this peace Jesus sometimes shows himself as a master to be looked on with awe, and sometimes as a father to be revered, and sometimes as a beloved spouse; and it keeps the soul in a wonderful reverence and in a loving gaze upon him, so that the soul is then well content, and never so well as then. For it feels such great security and rest in Jesus, and so much favor from his goodness, that it wants to be like this always and never do other work. It feels it is touching Jesus, and by virtue of that ineffable touch it is made whole and constant in itself. (2:24, 297)

This quiet prayer is touching the divinity rather than the humanity of Jesus. It is remaining with the divine presence, resting there, rather than actively meditating on Christ's human life. It is listening rather than speaking, obeying the psalmist's injunction, 'Be still and see that I am God' (Psalm 46:10, *Vulgate* 45:11). Reflecting on this passage, Hilton writes, 'You who are reformed in feeling ... cease sometimes from outward activity and see that I am God ... I, Jesus – God and man' (2:36, 270). In rest and stillness, gradually the likeness to Christ, whose recovery is the goal of the spiritual journey, is realized 'whole and constant' within.

Sometimes, in this quiet listening, 'various illuminations fall into the soul through grace.' Hilton calls these 'the sayings of Jesus and the sight of spiritual things', i.e., the sort of visionary experience we will find in Julian and Margery. He shies away from an explicit description of these intimate sights and sayings. But he does say the following:

You must know that all the trouble Jesus takes about a soul is in order to make it a true perfect spouse for himself in the height and fullness of love. Because that cannot be done at once, Jesus – who is love, and of all lovers the wisest – tries many ways before it can come about; and so that it can reach the fulfillment of true marriage he therefore uses such gracious speeches to a chosen soul in the guise of a suitor. He shows his jewels, giving many things and promising more, and offering courteous talk. Often he visits with much grace and spiritual comfort, as I have said before, but I do not know how to tell you in full detail how he does this. (2:44, 298)

For Hilton, Jesus is everything. Jesus is heaven:

What is heaven to a rational soul? Truly, nothing but Jesus, God. For if that only is heaven which is above everything, then God alone is heaven to the soul . . . for [God] alone is above the nature of a soul. Then if through grace a soul can have knowledge of that blessed nature of Jesus, [one] truly sees heaven, for [one] sees God. (2:33, 261)

This heaven, ultimate goal of the spiritual life, the full reform in feeling to the likeness of Christ, can be realized partially on earth through the graces of contemplation. It is the legacy of all the baptized.

5. THE THEOLOGIAN: JULIAN OF NORWICH

I saw two persons in bodily likeness, that is to say a lord and a servant; and with that God gave me spiritual understanding. The lord sits in state in rest and in peace. The servant stands before his lord, respectfully, ready to do his lord's will. The lord looks on his servant very lovingly and sweetly and mildly. He sends him to a certain place to do his will. Not only does the servant go, but he dashes off and runs at great speed, loving to do his lord's will. And soon he falls into a dell and is greatly injured; and then he groans and moans and tosses about and writhes, but he cannot rise or help himself in any way. And of all this, the greatest hurt which I saw him in was lack of consolation, for he could not turn his face to look on his loving lord, who was very close to him, in whom is all consolation; but like a man who was for the time extremely feeble and foolish, he paid heed to his feelings and his continuing distress . . . I looked carefully to know if I could detect any fault in him, or if the lord would impute to him any kind of blame; and truly none was seen, for the only cause of his falling was his good will and his great desire. And in spirit he was as prompt and as good as he was when he stood before his lord, ready to do his will. And all this time his loving lord looks on him most tenderly . . . with great compassion and pity.

Showings, Long Text, chapter 51[1]

This quotation is an example of the 'sight of spiritual things' which Hilton mentions as the fruit of contemplation at the end of *The Scale*. In 1373, its author, Julian of Norwich, received a

visionary experience in the midst of debilitating illness. Her
Showings, the book that resulted from this experience, is different from the writings we have studied so far. It is not merely
the record of personal religious experience, though that is
described in it. Nor is it specifically a guide for how to pray or
live the Christian life, though one might glean such instruction
from its pages. Rather Julian's *Showings* is an example of
theology as reflection on the experience of faith, revealing how
the insights born of contemplation can overflow into doctrinal
teaching. Julian is, more than anything else, a creative theologian with a bent toward speculative theology. In the Long
Text of *Showings* she covers all the main areas of Christian
doctrine: incarnation and redemption, ecclesiology, the one and
triune God, theological anthropology, creation and eschatology,
integrating them into a cohesive whole.[2] In the process she
gives witness to the interconnectedness between theology and
spirituality, showing that what one believes about God has a
profound effect on how one lives and prays and vice versa.

The above quotation is excerpted from the vision that forms
the centrepiece of Julian's *Showings*. Called the 'parable of the
lord and the servant', it resembles a medieval preacher's *exem-
plum*, a short story designed to illustrate the main point of a
sermon.[3] It functioned similarly for Julian, serving to clarify
aspects of her showings that puzzled her. Above all it provided
her with the image of a God who does not look on sinners with
wrath, but only with love. The parable thus held within it
a response to the momentous questions of sin, suffering and
salvation that preoccupied the fourteenth century. Julian never
mentions directly the disasters of her age,[4] but the message of
her revelations is obviously aimed at providing some cure for
the anxiety, confusion and guilt produced by the plague and
other fourteenth-century ills.

JULIAN THE VISIONARY

We know little about Julian's life, not even her given name,
since she probably adopted the name 'Julian' after the patron

saint of the church where she established her anchorhold. What slim knowledge we have comes from three sources: Julian's *Showings*, evidence found in wills, and the *Book* of Margery Kempe. The preface to the Short Text tells us that in 1413 Julian was still alive and living as a recluse in Norwich (i:125). This is corroborated by several wills found in the archives of Norwich Consistory Court, which leave money to a recluse named Julian in Norwich. Since the latest of these is dated 1416, we can safely assume that Julian lived at least until then.[5] We do not know when she was enclosed as an anchoress, but it was probably after the experience of 1373. Margery consulted her for advice, probably between 1411–13, indicating that by then Julian had gained some renown as a spiritual guide.[6]

From Julian herself we learn the year of her birth and the circumstances surrounding her visionary experience and the subsequent writing of *Showings*. Julian was born in 1342, since she received her visions in May 1373 when she was thirty and a half years old. She had fallen ill to the point of death, and had received the last rites. She recalls how in her youth she had prayed for three graces: to 'have mind' of the passion of Christ,[7] to be given a bodily sickness, and to be granted 'three wounds' of contrition, compassion, and longing for God (2:177). Such prayers were conventional expressions of piety in Julian's day, indicating her grounding in the tradition of affective devotion to Christ's passion and the Benedictine emphasis on compunction as the first step toward spiritual growth. The fact that Julian calls the feelings of compunction 'wounds' reveals her acquaintance with the 'wound of love' celebrated in bridal mysticism. We have seen the influence of all of these on Rolle, Hilton, and *The Cloud*. We have not found in them a prayer for bodily sickness, though the *Ancrene Wisse*, which Julian almost certainly knew, extols the spiritually healing effects of illness sent by God.[8] Julian's prayer may have been motivated by her knowledge of continental women visionaries, many of whom suffered chronic illness which they integrated into their spirituality as a way of sharing in the sufferings of Christ.[9]

In speaking of her prayer to 'have mind' of the passion, Julian mentions her desire for a 'bodily sight', a vision of the suffering Christ:

> I wished that I had been at that time with Magdalen and with the others who were Christ's lovers, so that I might have seen with my own eyes the Passion which our Lord suffered for me ... Therefore I desired a bodily sight, in which I might have more knowledge of our saviour's bodily pains, and of the compassion of our Lady and of all his true lovers who were living at that time and saw his pains, for I would have been one of them and suffered with them ... I wished afterwards, because of that revelation, to have truer [mind] of Christ's Passion. (2:177–8)

This desire for a 'bodily sight' also suggests Julian's awareness of continental women visionaries who flourished during the thirteenth and fourteenth centuries, and whose experiences were recorded in accounts of their visions.[10] We do not know if Julian had access to such writings before 1373, although she probably knew about the visionaries by word of mouth.[11] Julian has some things in common with these women, but she is unique in using her visions primarily as a springboard for creative theological speculation, something most visionaries did not do.[12]

Julian tells us that as she matured she forgot about her youthful prayer for illness and visions, repeating only her prayer for the wounds of contrition, compassion and longing for God. However, in the midst of her illness, which she doubtless understood as an answer to prayer, it occurred to her that she should pray for the second wound of compassion, so that she might unite her suffering to that of Christ. Much to her surprise, she received a vision of the Crucified. In her sickroom a curate had placed a crucifix before her eyes, and as she gazed at it:

> Suddenly I saw the red blood trickling down from under the crown, all hot, flowing freely and copiously, a living

stream, just as it seemed to me that it was at the time when the crown of thorns was thrust down upon his blessed head. Just so did he, both God and man, suffer for me . . . I was greatly astonished by this wonder and marvel, that he would so humbly be with a sinful creature living in this wretched flesh. I accepted it that at that time our Lord Jesus wanted, out of his courteous love, to show me comfort before my temptations began; for it seemed to me that I might well be tempted by devils, by God's permission and with his protection, before I died. (iii:129–30)

As is evident from this quotation, Julian shared with her contemporaries the fear of evil, of devils, of eternal damnation. The hour of death, in particular, was regarded as a time when the powers of evil would beset a soul most intensely, seeking to snatch it from the welcoming arms of God and drag it into the fires of hell.

At the beginning of *Showings* we see a young woman grappling first-hand with both the physical agony of dying and the mental anguish of fear, an experience that had been repeated thousands of times during the plague. And into the midst of this suffering comes the redemptive word of God. For Julian was saved from her physical agony: 'And suddenly . . . all my pain was taken from me and I was as sound . . . as ever I was before' (3:180). But much more important is her profound realization of the intensity of God's love for her, which drove all fear of eternal damnation from her mind forever: 'With this sight of his blessed passion, with the divinity . . . I knew well that this was strength enough for me, yes, and for all living creatures who were to be saved, against all the devils of hell and against all their spiritual enemies' (3:182).

Julian's was a personal experience of the essence of the Christian mystery of salvation. She realized in a concrete way the heart of the Christian message: that the event of Jesus Christ, culminating in his passion, death and resurrection, has conquered both sin and death, and that the power of God's grace abounds much more than the power of sin. She learned that a Christian who penetrates into the tremendous love of God for humanity and into the power of Christ's resurrected life simply cannot live in an attitude of scrupulous anxiety about sin or debilitating fear of eternal damnation, but rather in an attitude of awestruck joy over the loving God who only longs to save. This is the message of Julian's revelations. Into the atmosphere of sin, suffering and death of fourteenth-century England comes the reassuring word that God has compassion on that suffering, that indeed God has shared it all with the human race.

Julian tells us her showings came to her in three modes: bodily sights, spiritual sights, and words formed in her understanding.[13] By 'bodily sight' she means an imaginative vision, something like a dream image. Her experience is visual, lending a pictorial quality to her theological reflections. However, the visions were accompanied by 'spiritual sights' (deeper meanings beyond the visions), and words (heard not with her physical ears, but formed in her mind), which clarified the meaning of the visions. These spiritual sights and words contained the seeds of what would become her doctrinal teaching.

JULIAN THE THEOLOGIAN

Julian's *Showings* exists in two versions, the Short Text, written first, and the Long Text, a revision and expansion of the earlier one. We do not know when Julian wrote the Short Text; it has generally been assumed she did so shortly after the experience it describes, although this view has recently been challenged.[14] Julian does tell us something about the composition of the Long Text. In the Short Text she had hinted at her desire to write more about her showings, since there were aspects of them she could not comprehend (xxiii:167). She prayed for greater understanding, a prayer that was not answered for fifteen years, when she realized that 'Love' was the word summing up the message of her revelations (86:342). But it was not until five years later that Julian finally understood the parable of the lord and the servant, which affected her perception of all the revelations (51:270, 276). These insights suggested the need for a revision of her work, and resulted in the Long Text. In the period between her visionary experience and the recording of her final insights in the Long Text, Julian was doing what we call theology, a disciplined reflection upon the experience of faith in dialogue with the Christian tradition.

In her *Showings*, especially the Long Text, Julian demonstrates a degree of learning unusual for a woman of her day. She exhibits a firm grasp of Scripture, particularly the Pauline corpus, and a sophisticated understanding of classical Christian doctrine, especially the theology of Augustine, some of which was likely filtered through Victorine and Cistercian interpretation. She also shows familiarity with the English spiritual tradition, especially the *Ancrene Wisse* and Hilton's *Scale*. We are reduced to speculation when we attempt to explain how Julian achieved such learning. It is possible that she was a nun before being enclosed as an anchoress, but this would not explain her learning. While English convents in the early Middle Ages had been renowned centres of learning, this was no longer the case by the fourteenth century. Julian may have had a mentor – some monk, friar or cleric – who served as her spiritual director, and, recognizing her intelligence and eagerness to learn, became her tutor. There were abundant resources in Norwich for such a scenario. The cathedral was attached to a Benedictine priory which possessed one of the finest libraries in England, and the Franciscans, Dominicans, Augustinians, and Carmelites all had houses in Norwich – with libraries and learned men.[15]

It took courage for Julian to engage in the sort of theological speculation she does in *Showings*, with the intent to disseminate her work to others. The idea that women should not teach in the church is as old as Paul's first letter to the Corinthians (14:34), and the *Ancrene Wisse* warns explicitly against it:

[An anchoress], perhaps, is so learned or so wise in

speaking that she wants him who sits and speaks with her to know it ... And she who should be an anchoress becomes a teacher, and teaches him who has come to teach her. She wants to be recognized and known at once for her talk among the wise. Known she is – because on account of the very things for which she expects to be held wise, he understands she is a fool, since she hunts for praise and catches blame; for at the very least, when he has gone away, he will say, 'this anchoress talks a lot.' Eve in paradise held a long discussion with the serpent ... and so the enemy understood her weakness right away through her words, and found a way into her for her destruction. Our Lady St. Mary behaved quite differently: she did not discuss anything with the angel ... You, my beloved sisters, follow our Lady, and not the cackling Eve – because an anchoress, whatever she is, however much she knows, should keep quiet. She does not have the nature of a hen. The hen, when she has laid, can only cackle.[16]

It is no wonder that Julian should remark in the Short Text, 'But God forbid that you should say or assume that I am a teacher, for that is not and never was my intention; for I am a woman, ignorant, weak and frail.' Yet she believed God had entrusted her with a message for the benefit of others, so she continues, 'But because I am a woman, ought I therefore to believe that I should not tell you of the goodness of God, when I saw at that same time that it is his will that it be known?' (vi:135). The disclaimer about not being a teacher, however, is missing from the Long Text, implying that by then Julian had grown in confidence about her call and her ability to teach in God's name.

Julian's courage in publishing the theological conclusions drawn from her revelations is enhanced when viewed against the background of the prosecution of medieval heresy. In 1312 the Council of Vienne had issued the decree *Cum de quibusdam mulieribus* (*Concerning Certain Women*) in which it legitimated the investigation of women 'commonly known as beguines' who dared to 'discourse on the Trinity and the divine essence' and, in doing so, spread opinions contrary to the faith, leading simple folk into error under their pretence of sanctity.[17] The beguines were women who were experimenting with ways of living a common life centred on prayer, but bypassing many of the rules and regulations that governed religious orders of women, so as to be active in works of charity, particularly among the poor.[18] Many of their adherents were mystics and visionaries who became renowned for their holiness and piety, but, because of the unregulated nature of their lifestyle, they frequently were suspected of the so-called Free Spirit heresy. Julian was not a beguine, but any woman living an unregulated form of religious life, especially if she was suspected of preaching or teaching, could be investigated as a Free Spirit.[19]

There are indications in Julian's text that she may have been afraid of being accused of heresy.[20] One is struck, on reading *Showings*, how often Julian protests her loyalty to official church teaching. Such protestations occur most strongly where she is explaining the teachings drawn from her revelations regarding sin and salvation. To say, as Julian does, that God does not look upon the sinner with wrath, but only with love and compassion because of the suffering caused by sin (48–9:262–4), or that sin can actually become cause for glory rather than damnation (38:242–3), or that one ought not dwell overmuch upon one's past sins, but ought instead to give more attention to the love of God (79:334), could be interpreted as disregard for one's sinfulness, in a way similar to the claims of Free Spirits. Furthermore, Julian's understanding of God's promise 'all will be well' seemed to imply universal salvation, and to deny the existence of hell and purgatory, which the Free Spirits were thought to deny. Julian's persistent struggle to reconcile these points of her revelations with orthodox church teaching is highly detailed in sections of the Long Text, suggesting she may have known of cases where saying something similar was cause for suspicion. The growth and prosecution of popular Lollardy by the time Julian was composing *Showings* likely added to her concern.[21]

JULIAN'S TRINITARIAN THEOLOGY

The suffering Christ was the starting point for Julian's visionary experience, and for her theology as well. However, instead of focusing on the details of the passion, Julian is drawn to its deeper significance, which leads her immediately into the mystery of the Trinity. The link between the two is God's love; the passion of Christ is a concrete, graphic symbol of God's love for all humanity. Julian tells us,

> At the same time as I saw this [bodily] sight [of the head bleeding], our Lord showed me a spiritual sight of his familiar love ... He showed me something small, no bigger than a hazelnut, lying in the palm of my hand, and I perceived that it was as round as a ball. I looked at it and thought: What can this be? And I was given this general answer: It is everything which is made. I was amazed that it could last, for I thought that it was so little that it could suddenly fall into nothing. And I was answered in my understanding: It lasts and always will, because God loves it; and thus everything has being through the love of God. (iv:130)

Then Julian noticed a threefoldness to this love of God: 'In this little thing I saw three properties. The first is that God made it; the second is that he loves it; the third is that God preserves it. But what is that to me? It is that God is the Creator and the lover and the protector' (iv:131). The incipient trinitarian reference in this passage is greatly expanded in the Long Text into a fully-fledged theology of the economic Trinity.[22]

Like Hilton, Julian most often refers to the Trinity using the triad 'power, wisdom and love' and reflects on the human soul as image of the Trinity: 'For God is endless supreme truth [power], endless supreme wisdom, endless supreme love uncreated; and a human soul is a creature in God which has the same properties created' (44:256). However, instead of emphasizing how the natural faculties of the soul form a static trinitarian pattern, Julian focuses on how each soul gradually reproduces in itself God's actions in human history. God, the Source of all being, created the universe, sent forth the Word for its re-creation (in the incarnation), and sent forth the Spirit to return everything back into eschatological union with God. Each human soul is like God as *being* through its *creation* in God's image and likeness, effected by God's work of *nature*. But each soul is called to become more like God in its *re-creation* or *increase* over the course of a lifetime, through the action of God's *wisdom* in the work of *mercy*. Finally, each soul reaches its eschatological fulfilment through God's *love*, the work of *grace*. In this view, God is seen as always dynamically active in the lives of believers.

Since all of this was God's plan for humanity 'from before beginning', Julian intimates that the incarnation had a purpose other than repairing the damage caused by sin, and would have occurred even if there had been no sin:[23]

> Our reason is founded in God, who is nature's substance. From this substantial nature spring mercy and grace, and penetrate us, accomplishing everything for the fulfillment of our joy. These are our foundations, in which we have our being, our increase and our fulfillment ... For we cannot profit by our reason alone, unless we have equally memory and love; nor can we be saved merely because we have in God our natural foundation, unless we have, coming from the same foundation, mercy and grace ... For in our first making God gave us as much good and as great good as we could receive in our spirit alone; but his prescient purpose in his endless wisdom willed that we should be double. (56:290)

This way of viewing the incarnation places a positive value upon human life in time. God intended from the beginning that earthly existence would have a role to play in humanity's return to final glory.[24]

Julian applies names to God to describe the threefold operation of nature, mercy and grace. She frequently uses the triad 'maker, keeper, lover', drawn from her hazelnut vision. But in the Long Text she names 'three properties' to describe the same functions: 'the property of the fatherhood, the property of the motherhood, and the property of the lordship in one God' (58:293). In God's fatherhood, we have 'our protection and bliss, as regards our natural substance, which is ours by our creation' (58:293). In the motherhood of God, 'in knowledge and wisdom we have our perfection, as regards our sensuality, our restoration and our salvation' (58:293). In the lordship of God,

> we have our reward and our gift for our living and our labor, endlessly surpassing all that we desire . . . out of his plentiful grace . . . In the first we have our being, and in the second we have our increasing, and in the third we have our fulfillment. The first is nature, the second is mercy, the third is grace. (58:294)

Following classical trinitarian theology, Julian understands each of these works or properties as the operation of the one and only God. However, again consistent with the tradition, each work can be appropriated to a specific 'person' of the Trinity. Thus the property of fatherhood and the work of creation are appropriated to God the Source of all, the property of motherhood and the work of mercy to the Word of God, and the property of lordship and the work of grace to the Holy Spirit.

The theme of the economic Trinity functions as a general pattern for spiritual growth in Julian's theology. As for Hilton, her scriptural source may be Romans 8:30, the message of which is strikingly similar to hers: 'those whom [God] predestined he also called [the work of nature]; and those whom he called he also justified [the work of mercy]; and those whom he justified he also glorified [the work of grace].' However, unlike Hilton, Julian does not equate the steps of this progression with particular levels of spiritual development. In fact, in contrast to the authors we have examined thus far, Julian shows no interest at all in describing stages of spiritual progress or levels of perfection corresponding to various states of life. Her subject matter is God, the God she met in her visions, not religious experience as such. She learned that a true understanding of God as Love is the absolute foundation for the possibility of any authentic Christian life and prayer. Her life's work was an attempt to deepen her understanding of the message of her showings about the nature of this God, a message she felt called to disseminate to others, a message universal in its scope:

> Everything that I say about myself I mean to apply to all my fellow Christians, for I am taught that this is what our Lord intends in this spiritual revelation. And therefore I pray you all for God's sake, and I counsel you for your own profit, that ... you contemplate God, who out of his courteous love and his endless goodness was willing to show this vision generally, to the comfort of us all. (vi:133)

Prayer always contains an element of self-donation, an acknowledgement of the need for a 'higher power' to come to one's aid. But such an act of self-donation or expression of need can only be done from an attitude of trust. Thus one's image of God is absolutely crucial. If one imagines God as a stern judge, distant and far away, difficult to please, such an attitude of trust is practically impossible. But if one imagines God as someone who loves unconditionally, no matter how much one sins, then it is possible to approach God in trust, expecting to be accepted and helped. Julian realized that her age's preoccupation with sin and eternal damnation was due to a lack of appreciation of the intensity of God's love for humanity:

> Some of us believe that God is almighty and may do everything, and that God is all wisdom and can do everything, but that God is all love and wishes to do everything, there we fail, and it is this ignorance which most hinders God's lovers ... For [God's] love makes power and wisdom very humble to us; for just as by God's courtesy he forgets our sin from the time that we repent, just so does he wish us to forget our sin with regard to our unreasonable depression and our doubtful fears. (73:323)

It is such a trustworthy God that Julian met in her revelations, changing her perspective forever.

GOD'S MOTHERLY AND HOMELY LOVE

The theme of the motherhood of God has been forgotten in modern times, but throughout the Middle Ages, particularly in devotional literature, it was quite common. It usually took the shape of devotion to Jesus as Mother, in which three analogies were drawn between Jesus' saving activity and certain aspects of motherhood. Just as a mother brings her child to birth through pains of labour, so Christ brought humanity to new birth through his sufferings on the cross. Just as a mother nourishes her child with food from her body, so Christ nourishes Christians through the sacraments, especially the eucharist. Just as a mother cares for her child with love and compassion, so Christ loves and cares for those made God's children through baptism. All of these analogies are present in Julian's description of Jesus as Mother, but she goes beyond them. Motherhood for her expresses the very essence, not merely certain incidental aspects of Christ's activity towards humanity, summarizing the whole doctrine of salvation.[25]

For Julian, the eternal bond of love existing between God and humanity is focused on the second person of the Trinity, God's Word and Wisdom, the perfect image of God in whom and through whom all were created. Her primary source for this is doubtless the all-pervasive Augustinian trinitarian tradition but it could also have scriptural roots. Paul identifies Christ as God's wisdom, realized, paradoxically, through the folly of the cross: 'For Jews demand signs and Greeks desire wisdom, but we proclaim Christ crucified, a stumbling block to Jews and foolishness to Gentiles, but to those who are the called, both Jews and Greeks, Christ the power of God and the wisdom of God' (1 Corinthians 1:22–4).

Julian may also have meditated upon the Jewish Scriptures, where Wisdom (*Sophia*) is imaged as a female figure, existing before the beginning of the world, who is associated with all of

God's activities vis-à-vis the world: creation, salvation, sanctification.[26] In the early Church this Wisdom figure was identified with Christ and used in the development of the doctrines of the incarnation and Trinity. The book of Wisdom calls her the 'mother' of 'all good things' (7:11–12), an idea even more beautifully expressed in the Latin Vulgate's version of the book of Sirach, where Wisdom herself announces, 'I am mother of fair love, of fear and knowledge and holy hope. In me is all grace of the way and of the truth, in me all hope of life and virtue' (Ecclesiasticus 24:24–5). Julian reflects in a similar vein: 'The deep wisdom of the trinity is our mother, in whom we are enclosed' (54:285).

Elsewhere in the Jewish Scriptures, the prophet Isaiah compares God to an earthly mother: 'Can a woman forget her nursing child, or show no compassion for the child of her womb? Even these may forget, yet I will not forget you' (Isaiah 49:15). Julian's own description of Christ as Mother is an elaboration of this analogy:

> We know that all our mothers bear us for pain and for death ... But our true Mother Jesus, he alone bears us for joy and for endless life ... The mother may sometimes suffer the child to fall and to be distressed in various ways, for its own benefit, but she can never suffer any kind of peril to come to her child, because of her love. And though our earthly mother may suffer her child to perish, our heavenly Mother Jesus may never suffer us who are his children to perish. (60:297–8; 61:300–1)

While Julian most frequently associates the image of mother with Jesus, she also has a sense of the motherhood of God as such. God can be said to be our Mother in God's threefold trinitarian function: 'I understand three ways of contemplating motherhood in God. The first is the foundation of our nature's creation; the second is his taking of our nature, where the motherhood of grace begins; the third is the motherhood at work, ... and it is all one love' (59:297). In other words, God as such is our Mother, operating in the works of creation, redemption, and sanctification.

Julian applies her teaching about God as Mother to the life of prayer. Knowledge of one's sinfulness can keep one from God and greatly hinder the prayer of trust. However, if one imagines God as a mother, one's reaction might be different:

> When our falling and our wretchedness are shown to us, we are so much afraid ... But then our courteous Mother does not wish us to flee away ... but wants us to behave like a child. For when it is distressed and frightened, it runs quickly to its mother, and if it can do no more, it calls to the mother for help with all its might. So [God] wants us to act as a meek child, saying: My kind Mother, my gracious Mother, my beloved Mother, have mercy on me. I have made myself filthy and unlike you, and I may not and cannot make it right except with your help and grace. (61:301)

Consequently, one of the virtues most deeply prized by Julian is the virtue of humility or spiritual childhood, which she understood in a way similar to what we found in *The Cloud* and Hilton, as the expression of creaturehood.

The image of God as Mother emphasizes, for Julian, God's contentment to be at home with humanity, which she calls the 'homeliness' (intimacy or familiarity) of God's love. We are God's home, an idea most evident in the fact of the incarnation: human reality is the place where God chose to dwell. Several images from the parable of the lord and the servant spell out this idea. Christ as servant appears in Adam's tunic, representing the nature he shares with all humanity, which, as a result of his life, death and resurrection, is 'made lovely by our savior, new, white and bright and forever clean' (51:278). Further, humanity was meant to be 'God's city and dwelling place', and when sin made that city unfit for God, the lord sat on the bare ground until the servant had restored it (51:272). Once restored, it becomes God's favourite dwelling place, God's 'homeliest home' (68:313). Collectively, this city is Christ's

Church in whom Christ dwells as head (51:278),[27] but it also represents the individual soul in whom 'the blessed trinity our creator dwells eternally' (1:177).

Julian's emphasis on humanity, Church, the earth or history as God's home gives her *Showings* a different atmosphere from what we have seen in Rolle, *The Cloud,* and Hilton. Each of them devoted many pages to spelling out the evils of the world, the need for strict custody of the senses to ward off temptation, and especially the need to banish all thoughts of worldly things from the mind in order to reach union with God. The absence of such warnings is glaring in Julian's text. She sometimes uses the phrase 'wretched world' or 'wretched flesh', both commonplaces in her day, to refer to the effects of sin on earthly reality. She does warn against seeking one's ultimate rest in anything created: 'Our hearts and souls are not in perfect ease, because here we seek rest in this thing which is so little, in which there is no rest, and we do not know our God who is almighty, all wise and all good, for [God] is true rest ... Everything which is beneath [God] is not sufficient for us' (5:183–4). But for Julian, the created universe is fundamentally good, and reveals God. She describes the proper Christian attitude towards the world as one of 'endlessly marvelling at the greatness of God, the creator, and at the smallest part of all that is created' (75:327), an attitude that will remain even in heaven. Since the world is God's home, escape from created reality to find God is foreign to Julian's spirituality.

On the other hand, the homeliness of God's love means that God is our home, within whom we dwell. We are enclosed in God our Mother as in a womb: 'our savior is our true Mother, in whom we are endlessly born and out of whom we shall never come' (57:292). In a stunning passage, Julian uses the analogy of clothing to express the closeness of God to humanity: 'I saw that [God] is to us everything which is good and comforting for our help. He is our clothing, who wraps and enfolds us for love, embraces us and shelters us, surrounds us for his love; which is so tender that he may never desert us' (5:183). Julian's words tumble over each other in her eagerness to express this idea adequately:

> For as the body is clad in the cloth, and the flesh in the skin, and the bones in the flesh, and the heart in the trunk, so are we, soul and body, clad and enclosed in the goodness of God. Yes, and more closely, for all these vanish and waste away; the goodness of God is always complete, and closer to us, beyond any comparison. (6:186)

The God of love has been humanity's home from all eternity, 'our natural place, in which we were created by the motherhood of love, a mother's love which never leaves us' (60:297). The human soul has been 'treasured and hidden in God, known and loved from without beginning, . . . preciously knitted to God in its making' (53:284). The homeliness of Julian's images – mother and child, clothing, knitting – serve to underline the fundamental domesticity of God's relationship to humanity.

'ALL WILL BE WELL' – SEEING WITH GOD'S EYES

The predominant movement in the writings of Rolle, *The Cloud* author, and, to a lesser extent, Hilton, with their focus on various stages of 'ascent' to God, is upward, from us to God. This is true even though all of them state, quite correctly, that God must first approach us through grace to enable such an ascent. Still, in this approach, God seems 'out there' somewhere, far away, 'up there' in heaven, and one must gradually put the world firmly behind in order to reach union with God. The emphasis is upon God's transcendence. By contrast, the predominant movement in Julian's *Showings* is downward, from God to us. Although she may well have practised the steps recommended by the other authors, she does not mention them. Instead she writes about the unexpected gift God gave her in her revelations, the focus of which is God's nearness to us. The emphasis is on God's immanence.

However, this does not mean that Julian ignores God's transcendence, an idea colourfully expressed in her use of the word

'courteous' to describe God's love, calling up the image of a high
and mighty lord.[28] Julian has an acute sense that however near
God may be to us, nevertheless God's ways are not our ways,
and there remains a profound mystery about God which we will
never understand completely.

The difference between God's perspective and that of humans
was brought home most clearly to Julian with respect to sin. In
an extraordinary vision, she is privileged for a moment to see
things from God's point of view:

> I saw God in a [point], that is to say in my understanding,
> by which vision I saw that he was present in all things. I
> contemplated it carefully, seeing and recognizing through
> it that he does everything which is done. I marvelled at
> that vision with a gentle fear, and I thought: What is sin?
> For I saw truly that God does everything, ... and I was
> certain that he does no sin. (11:197–8)

As a result of this Julian later concludes, along with countless
theologians before her, that 'sin is no deed, ... no kind of substance, no share in being' (27:225). As the absence of good, sin
is nothing. In the same vision, Julian realizes the profound
difference between how humans and God look at sin:

> [We regard] some deeds as well done and some as evil, and
> our Lord does not regard them so, for everything which
> exists in nature is of God's creation, so that everything
> which is done has the property of being God's doing ... I
> saw most truly that [God] never changed his purpose in
> any kind of thing, nor ever will eternally. For there was
> nothing unknown to him in his just ordinances before time
> began, and therefore all things were set in order, before
> anything was made, as it would endure eternally. And no
> kind of thing will fail in that respect, for he has made
> everything totally good. (11:198–9)

The kernel of this revelation was later encapsulated in the
phrase for which Julian is so famous: 'All will be well' (27:225).

This vision was a source of confusion to Julian because it

seemed to contradict everything she had learned about sin and damnation from church teaching. She also knew, probably from personal experience, how much humans suffer from sin, either their own or that of others. To Julian, God seems to dismiss sin far too lightly. Throughout her revelations she persists in worrying and questioning God about sin, finally praying: 'Ah, good Lord, how could all things be well, because of the great harm which has come through sin to your creatures? And here I wished ... for some plainer explanation through which I might be at ease about this matter' (29:227). The 'plainer explanation' was provided in the parable of the lord and the servant. However, this explanation was hardly 'plain' to Julian's understanding. In fact, it was so unclear that Julian did not even include it in the Short Text, and it took her twenty years to unpack its meaning.

In the parable the servant stands lovingly before his lord, runs eagerly to do the lord's bidding, but falls into a ditch and cannot complete the task. Julian initially thought the vision was a metaphor for the fall, and that the servant represented Adam understood as all humanity. However, the servant does not seem to be responsible for the fall, which seems like an unhappy accident. Furthermore, the lord, representing God, does not look upon the servant with blame, only with compassion. Both ideas clearly seem to contradict church teaching.[29] Eventually Julian reaches a new level of understanding, realizing that the servant represents both Adam and Christ:

> When Adam fell, God's Son fell; because of the true union which was made in heaven, God's Son could not be separated from Adam, for by Adam I understand all [humankind]. Adam fell from life to death, into the valley of this wretched world, and after that into hell. God's Son fell with Adam, into the valley of the womb of the maiden ... and that was to excuse Adam from blame ... In all this our good Lord showed his own Son and Adam as only one man ... And so has our good Lord Jesus taken

upon him all our blame; and therefore our Father may
not . . . assign more blame to us than to his own beloved
Son Jesus Christ. (51:274–5)

In other words, from God's eternal vantage point, the fact of
human sin is never viewed apart from its remedy in the incarnation. Because of the union that exists between Christ and
humanity, whenever God looks at any of us, even in our sin,
God sees Christ. What human beings see as process, and interpret in terms of time sequence or cause and effect, is seen as
eternally accomplished by God. From God's perspective, sin is
overcome, humanity is God's dwelling place, and all is well.

A related aspect of her revelations that Julian cannot ignore
is their strong suggestion, implied in the phrase 'All will be
well', that everyone will in the end be saved by the triumph of
God's love. Julian knew that such teaching was heresy and
she labours mightily throughout *Showings* to reconcile it with
orthodox doctrine. In doing so she turns to the essential difference between human experience in time, which legitimizes
church teaching about sin and the possibility of eternal damnation, and God's eternal perspective which remains
mysterious to us:

> It seemed to me that it was necessary to see and to know
> that we are sinners and commit many evil deeds which we
> ought to forsake, and leave many good deeds undone which
> we ought to do, so that we deserve pain, blame and wrath.
> And despite all this, I saw truly that our Lord was never
> angry, and never will be . . . There are many hidden mys-
> teries which can never be known until the time when God
> in his goodness has made us worthy to see them. (46:259)

She suggests the possibility of some further act on the part of
God, kept secret from us, whereby all those considered damned
by the Church will somehow be saved at the end of time. With
this rather unsatisfactory solution Julian rests content.[30]

If Julian's teaching can be summed up in one word, that word
is love. Her whole effort is to present to her troubled times the

picture of an absolutely loving God. She ends her *Showings* with this word 'love':

> I was taught that love is our Lord's meaning. And I saw very certainly in this and in everything that before God made us he loved us, which love was never abated and never will be. And in this love he has done all his works, and in this love he has made all things profitable to us, and in this love our life is everlasting. In our creation we had beginning, but the love in which he created us was in him from without beginning. In this love we have our beginning and all this shall we see in God without end. (86:342–3)

6. THE PILGRIM: MARGERY KEMPE

Then they went to the Church of the Holy Sepulchre in Jerusalem ... The friars lifted up a cross and led the pilgrims about from one place to another where our Lord had suffered his pains and his Passion, every man and woman carrying a wax candle in one hand. And the friars always, as they went about, told them what our Lord suffered in every place. And this creature wept and sobbed as plenteously as though she had seen our Lord with her bodily eyes suffering his Passion at that time ... And when they came up on to the Mt. of Calvary, she fell down because she could not stand or kneel, but writhed and wrestled with her body, spreading her arms out wide, and cried with a loud voice as though her heart would have burst apart, for in the city of her soul she saw truly and freshly how our Lord was crucified. Before her face she heard and saw in her spiritual sight the mourning of our Lady, of St. John and Mary Magdalene, and of many others that loved our Lord.

The Book of Margery Kempe, book 1, chapter 28[1]

The pious laywoman Margery Kempe is in many ways unlike the other English mystics, for she lived out her call to holiness neither in monastery nor anchorhold but in the world. Literally a pilgrim, she travelled the length and breadth of England and beyond to pray at the most famous Christian shrines. But she was also a pioneer forging the uncharted path of combining her status as laywoman, wife and mother with the call to contemplation. Margery was forced by circumstance, more often than

not, to practise her devotions publicly. Thus her intense compassion for the suffering of Christ was witnessed by everyone
around her, whether or not they were willing participants. Her
outbursts of crying at any mention of the passion of Christ were
annoying, to say the least, to those around her. As a result, she
was the victim of misunderstanding and abuse.

Margery's story gives us a sense of how difficult it was to step
outside the accepted patterns of holiness sanctioned in her day.
The highest level of Christian perfection demanded virginity, a
condition not achievable for the mother of fourteen children.
Margery struggled for much of her life with feelings of inad-
equacy, doubting the legitimacy of her visionary experiences,
constantly seeking religious experts to verify their authenticity. Gradually, as she grew in spiritual maturity, she learned
to trust her experience, and received the consolation of
knowing she was precious to God in spite of her loss of virginity.
Margery puts us in touch with the extent to which the kind of
hierarchical ordering of the religious life, as described by Rolle
and *The Cloud* author, could be problematic for someone living
in the world. Even Hilton, who endorsed the possibility of a life
of perfection for all the baptized, probably never envisioned the
extremes to which Margery's unique vocation led her. Julian,
however, reassured Margery that her experiences were from
God, counselling her: 'set all your trust in God and do not fear
the talk of the world' (1:18, 78).

Margery's call to holiness simply did not fit the patterns of
religious living considered appropriate in her milieu, a fact
made apparent by the reactions of various people to her. When
she first approaches Richard Caister, the vicar of St Stephen's
in Norwich, asking to speak with him for an hour or two about
the love of God, his reply is condescending: 'Bless us! How could
a woman occupy one or two hours with the love of our Lord?'
(1:17, 74). She is counselled by those who pity her because of
the abuse she suffers: 'Woman, give up this life that you lead,
and go and spin, and card wool, as other women do' (1:53, 168).
In one telling passage, an irritated monk remarks, 'I wish you
were enclosed in a house of stone, so that no one should speak

with you' (1:13, 63), implying that the sort of life Margery was attempting to lead belonged in an anchoress's cell.

The history of Margery's *Book* attests to the strangeness of her lifestyle. Before the discovery of the entire manuscript in 1934, the only sections of the text in circulation were seven pages of extracts from her more conventional visions in which she is identified as an 'anchoress of Lynn'.[2] No one imagined that a woman living in the world would have such experiences and thoughts.

If Margery's lifestyle defies accepted categories, the same might be said of her *Book,* which has some things in common with hagiographical accounts of women saints, but is generally too idiosyncratic in its details to fall into that genre.[3] Nor is it a work of spiritual guidance. It is actually the first extant autobiography in the English language, but autobiography in a limited sense when judged by modern standards. Primarily the story of Margery's relationship with God, it ignores details of her life not associated directly with her spiritual development. Consistent with medieval ideas of autobiography, Margery as protagonist is not the primary agent, but God assumes that role in the creation of her 'self'. Thus, throughout her *Book,* Margery refers to herself in the third person as 'this creature', God's creation.[4]

MARGERY'S LIFE AND *BOOK*

Margery was born around 1373, the daughter of a prominent citizen of King's Lynn in Norfolk. Her father, John Brunham, served five times as mayor and represented the city as one of its two Members of Parliament at least six times over a twenty-year period (1364–84). Margery's family belonged to the newly emergent wealthy middle class, with members in the merchant guild of the Holy Trinity, which played a leading role in both the economic and political affairs of Lynn. Margery took pride in her family's status, as evidenced by her response to her husband's efforts to restrain her 'proud ways': 'She answered sharply and shortly, and said that she was come of worthy kindred ... And therefore she would keep up the honour of her kindred, whatever anyone said' (1:2, 44). Because of her family's position, it is somewhat odd that Margery was illiterate, since by the fifteenth century, women of her class usually did learn to read.[5]

Her family's influence helps to explain Margery's forceful personality, and may also have afforded her protection from prominent officials when she got into trouble. Throughout her *Book,* Margery is invited to dine with bishops and abbots, who treat her with respect. For example, when Margery passes through Worcester on her journey to Spain, she is invited to meet with the bishop there who greets her with the words, 'Margery ... I know well enough you are John of Brunham's daughter from Lynn.' He then provides lodging for her in his house until her ship is ready to sail (1:45, 146–7).

When she was twenty, Margery married John Kempe, whose family is mentioned in the Lynn city records, but was not of the same stature as the Brunham family. The two seem to have had a good relationship. Throughout her *Book* Margery has nothing but good to say of John, 'who always had tenderness and compassion for her' (1:1, 43) and 'was always a good and easygoing man with her ... [who] spoke up for her as much as he dared' (1:15, 68). Although they lived apart after their mutual vow of celibacy, Margery cared for John during the last years of his life, after he was paralysed by a fall.

Shortly after her marriage, 'as nature would have it', Margery became pregnant with the couple's first child. It was a difficult pregnancy, and Margery was so ill that she feared death. She sent for her confessor, hoping to unburden herself of a sin she had kept hidden, but the priest was so unsympathetic and impatient with her hesitant efforts to confess, that she was unable to do so. Margery cites this experience as the primary reason for the madness that afflicted her for eight months after the birth of her child. She experienced horrible visions of devils attempting to devour her, and was so violent towards herself and others that she had to be forcibly restrained. She was cured by a vision of Jesus who appeared to her 'in the likeness of a man, the most seemly, most beauteous, and most amiable that ever might be seen ... clad in a mantle of purple silk, sitting upon her bedside, looking upon her with so blessed a countenance that she was strengthened in all her spirits.' He said simply, 'Daughter why have you forsaken me, and I never forsook you?' (1:1, 42). Margery immediately regained her wits and asked for the keys to the buttery, resuming her household duties.

Although this vision of Christ afforded Margery consolation and healing, it did not effect a complete conversion from her arrogant ways. She confesses to conceit regarding her appearance, pride in her family connections, contempt for her husband's lower social status, envy of her neighbours, desire for their admiration, and covetousness for worldly goods. In order to amass more wealth, she attempted several business ventures – brewing and milling – both of which failed miserably. This period lasted at least four years, probably longer, after her recovery. But eventually Margery experienced a genuine conversion from her worldliness, after which she engaged in a life of penance, prayer and good works for others. After about twenty years of marriage, during which she bore fourteen children, Margery persuaded her husband to agree to her long-cherished desire for celibacy, which gave her the freedom to pursue her religious life in earnest. She experienced many 'high contemplations' of Christ, his mother and other saints, and travelled far and wide, to hear gifted preachers and to visit famous shrines in England. She travelled abroad, first to the Holy Land, Assisi and Rome, then to St James of Compostela in Spain, and finally to Germany.

In the Holy Land, Margery began wailing loudly at any mention of the passion, and began wearing white clothing at Christ's command. When she returned to England her unusual behaviour attracted much attention, and she was arrested and questioned for heresy on several occasions (1:46–55).[6] Each time she was exonerated, her accusers acknowledging 'she knows her faith well enough' (1:52, 163). In her trial before the Archbishop of York, when she was accused of preaching, she answered somewhat defiantly, 'I do not preach, sir; I do not go into any pulpit. I use only conversation and good words, and that I will do while I live' (1:52, 164). She eventually secured a letter from the Archbishop of Canterbury attesting to her orthodoxy, which saved her from further prosecution (1:55, 175).

About twenty-five years after her conversion, Margery attempted to record the story of her life and visions. Her first amanuensis wrote badly in a combination of German and English that was almost indecipherable, and died before the work was completed. Margery thereafter engaged a priest to complete the task. After many delays and several bouts of reluctance on his part, he succeeded in rewriting the entire first book under Margery's direction. In 1438 he began a second book, much shorter than the first, again under Margery's guidance. Although one cannot be certain of the extent to which these scribes added their own interpretative comments, the *Book* is generally understood by scholars to be Margery's own. Her forceful, exuberant personality dominates its pages.

We know nothing about the early circulation of Margery's *Book*. It exists in a single manuscript copy discovered in 1934 in the home of William Butler-Bowdon. Believed to be an early copy of the original, it once belonged to the library of the Carthusian monastery of Mount Grace in Yorkshire.

MARGERY'S SPIRITUAL JOURNEY

Margery's *Book* is not meant to be a work of spiritual guidance. However, a discerning eye can detect in the story of her life a movement analogous to the purgative, illuminative and unitive ways described by earlier writers.[7] Margery's life is a progression from turbulence to peace, marked by transformative experiences that she cites as turning-points in her spiritual maturation.

The first of these was her conversion itself, an experience reminiscent of Rolle's opening of the heavenly door, in which she became aware of the joy that exists in heaven:

One night, as this creature lay in bed with her husband, she heard a melodious sound so sweet and delectable that she thought she had been in paradise. And immediately she jumped out of bed and said, 'Alas that ever I sinned! It is full merry in heaven.' This melody was so sweet that . . . it caused this creature . . . to shed very plentiful and abundant tears of high devotion, with great sobbings, and sighings for the bliss of heaven. (1:3, 46)

After this Margery began a life of penance, as classical an example of the purgative way to be found anywhere. She fasted, kept long vigils, confessed her sins two or three times a day, wore a hair-shirt, and wept copiously out of sorrow for her sins. She lost all desire for sexual intercourse with her husband and began longing for a life of celibacy. For about two years she lived this way in 'great quiet of spirit', followed by 'three years of great temptations', the most severe and humiliating of which was a sexual attraction to a man other than her husband (1:4, 48–50).

The next turning-point in Margery's spiritual development happened when she received from Christ the consolation that he had forgiven her sins 'to the uttermost point', along with the promise that she would 'never come into hell nor into purgatory . . . but have the bliss of heaven.' She is counselled to replace her hair-shirt with 'a hair-shirt in [her] heart' which Christ would give her, to abstain from meat, to receive communion every Sunday, and to take as her confessor a Dominican anchorite, a doctor of divinity in Lynn, to whom she was to confide all her religious experiences. She is also encouraged to give up vocal prayer in favour of quiet meditation: 'You shall lie still and speak to me in thought, and I shall give you high meditation and true contemplation' (1:5, 52). This marks a new phase of Margery's spiritual journey, resembling the illuminative way.

When Margery asks Christ what she should 'think about', he responds, 'think of my mother', and Margery does so, beginning with Mary's birth. Consistent with her vocation of motherhood perfected through long practice, Margery 'busied herself to take the child to herself and look after her until she was twelve years of age, with good food and drink, with fair white clothing and white kerchiefs' (1:6, 52–3). In her imagination she hears Mary tell of the annunciation, and goes with her to visit Elizabeth. Then she accompanies Mary to Bethlehem, where she 'procured lodgings for her every night . . . and begged for our Lady pieces of fair white cloth and kerchiefs to swaddle her son in.' When Jesus was born,

> she arranged bedding for our Lady to lie on with her blessed son. And later she begged food for our Lady and her blessed child. Afterwards she swaddled him, weeping bitter tears of compassion, mindful of the painful death that he would suffer for the love of sinful [people], saying to him, 'Lord I shall treat you gently; I will not bind you tightly. I pray you not to be displeased with me.' (1:6, 53–4)

In these meditations, Margery draws upon domestic duties familiar to her as a mother, and offers them in service first to the baby Mary and then to the infant Christ. They are the sort of meditations only a mother would likely conceive. Margery never mentions her own children, apart from recounting the story of one grown son (2:1–2, 265–9). But these meditations provide a glimpse into the sort of mother she must have been, revealing a tender but practical and efficient side to her personality. These meditations must have made Margery feel confident to approach Mary and Christ, tapping into her skills, reassuring her that she has something to give, even though she is not a virgin. In one meditation Mary thanks her: 'I am well pleased with your service' (1:6, 53), as does Christ: 'I thank you for as many times as you have bathed me, in your soul, at home in your chamber' (1:86, 255). One wonders about Margery's silence regarding her own children, and is tempted to think they represented for her something unconnected with what she considered her authentic spiritual life focused explicitly upon her relationship with God. Did she ever see her service to them as service to Christ? She never says so. Later in her book she reveals that whenever she sees a mother with a male child, she is reminded of the infant Jesus (cf. 1:35, 123; 39, 131; 82, 239; 83, 241). One wonders if she ever thought of her own children in the same light.

In a second series of meditations, Margery accompanies Mary through the events of Christ's passion. She watches Christ bid his mother farewell: 'Then our Lord took up his mother in his arms and kissed her very sweetly, and said to her, "Ah, blessed mother, be cheered and comforted . . . Bless me and let me go to do my father's will" ' (1:79, 228–9). Margery then imagines that she and Mary follow Jesus, witnessing all the sufferings he experienced. Here her meditations are reflective of the graphic description present in the passion meditations of Rolle and others, and visible in the artwork Margery would have seen in the churches she visited. For example, in Norwich cathedral there is a late-fourteenth-century retable which represents the flagellation scene with Christ's arms tied above his head to a pillar as he is whipped by torturers.[8] Margery's meditation reads: 'She saw in her contemplation our Lord Jesus Christ bound to a pillar, and his hands were bound above his head. And then she saw sixteen men with sixteen scourges, and each scourge had eight tips of lead on the end, and each tip was full of sharp prickles . . . And those men . . . made a covenant that each of them should give our Lord forty strokes' (1:80, 231).

At the crucifixion, when the cross was raised, 'our Lord's body shook and shuddered, and all the joints of that blissful body burst and broke apart, and his precious blood ran down with rivers of blood on every side' (1:80, 233). When Jesus died,

> she thought she saw our Lady swoon and fall down and lie still, as if she had been dead. Then this creature thought that she ran all round the place like a mad woman, crying and roaring . . . She came to our Lady . . . saying to her . . . 'Lady, cease from your sorrowing . . . I will sorrow for you, for your sorrow is my sorrow.' (1:80, 234)

After Jesus was laid in the tomb, Margery accompanied Mary

to her home, where 'she made for our Lady a good hot drink of gruel and spiced wine' (1:81, 236). Margery remained with Mary and was there on the third day when Jesus came and 'took up his blessed mother and kissed her very sweetly', saying, 'Dear mother, my pain is all gone, and now I shall live for ever more' (1:81, 237).

Through Mary, Margery witnesses Christ's passion from a viewpoint that may have been natural to her, the viewpoint of a mother enduring the death of a child. One wonders how many of Margery's offspring died as children, a happening quite common in the fifteenth century. Once again, Margery may be drawing upon something familiar to her, and using that experience as her entry into prayer. Unlike Julian, Margery never thinks of Christ as her mother; rather she, together with Mary, mothers Christ.

Margery thrived on these emotion-filled meditations on Christ's humanity, which became even more vivid and real to her as a result of her pilgrimage to the Holy Land. She undertook this journey immediately after beginning to live as a celibate, and it marks another turning-point in her religious life. It enabled her to enter a sort of 'liminal space', in which the ordinary familial and societal restrictions governing her life were lifted, permitting her the freedom to explore new options.[9] Margery's motivation was simply to see and touch the memorials of Christ's life, to walk where he walked, see what he saw, as a way of deepening her devotion to his humanity. It enabled her to participate more fully in the events of Christ's life and death, and as such was a form of mystical experience for her. As Atkinson makes clear, 'the mystic and the pilgrim are not separate or separable in Margery Kempe.' Pilgrimage was, for her, a form of 'exteriorized mysticism', fully consistent with the public nature of her vocation.[10]

Through her meditations on Christ's life and experiences of the holy places, Margery grew in familiarity with Christ, becoming comfortable with that same 'homeliness' of God which Julian spoke of. But in one meditation she witnesses the scene where Jesus appears to Mary Magdalene after the resurrection: 'Our Lord said to her, "Touch me not." Then this creature thought that Mary Magdalene said to our Lord, "Ah, Lord, I see you don't want me to be as homely with you as I have been before," and looked very miserable' (1:81, 238). Margery tells us her reaction:

> If our Lord had spoken to her as he did to Mary, she thought she could never have been happy. That was when ... he said, "Touch me not." This creature had such grief and sorrow at those words that, whenever she heard them in any sermon ... she wept, sorrowed and cried ... for the love and desire that she had to be with our Lord. (1:81, 238)

We know that Margery was familiar with 'Hilton's book', and she may well have been remembering Hilton's use of this same Gospel story at the end of *The Scale* as encouragement to move from meditation on Christ's humanity to a contemplation of his divinity.[11] The next turning-point in Margery's spiritual journey is an invitation to do just that.

Subsequent to her visit to the Holy Land, Margery travels to Rome, where she experiences a mystical marriage to 'the Godhead'. After telling her he is 'well pleased' with her because of her faithfulness to the sacraments and her compassion for Christ's suffering, God the Father proposes to Margery: 'I will have you wedded to my Godhead, because I shall show you my secrets and my counsels, for you shall live with me without end.' Margery's response is silence 'because she was very much afraid of the Godhead ... for all her love and affection were fixed on the manhood of Christ, and ... she ... would not be parted from that for anything' (1:35, 122–3). It had been Christ in his humanity who came to her and offered her healing in the midst of her madness and fear of damnation. He was her way into a non-threatening relationship with God, and it is not surprising that she is loath to leave behind the comfort she feels from this relationship. 'The Godhead' seems remote, mysterious and threatening, perhaps reviving her earlier fear of

God at the realization of her sinfulness. None the less, the marriage takes place:

> And then the Father took her by the hand [spiritually] in her soul, before the Son and the Holy Ghost, and the Mother of Jesus, and all the twelve apostles, and St. Katherine and St. Margaret and many other saints and holy virgins, with a great multitude of angels, saying to her soul, 'I take you, Margery, for my wedded wife, for fairer, for fouler, for richer, for poorer, provided that you are humble and meek in doing what I command you to do. For, daughter, there was never a child so kind to its mother as I shall be to you, both in joy and sorrow, to help you and comfort you. And that I pledge to you.' And then the Mother of God and all the saints that were present there in her soul prayed that they might have much joy together. (1:35, 123–4)

God the Father eliminates Margery's fear, interestingly, by promising to be as kind to her as a child is to its mother. Once again, the image of the mother/child relationship aids Margery's spiritual growth.

In her mystical marriage Margery revisits the merriment in heaven which she had noted in her conversion experience. Now she finds herself included in it, with all the saints and angels celebrating her marriage to the Godhead. While Margery was still living with her husband, grieving the loss of her virginity, she had prayed,

> Ah, Lord, maidens are now dancing merrily in heaven. Shall I not do so? Because I am no virgin, lack of virginity is now great sorrow to me. I think I wish I had been killed as soon as I was taken from the font, so that I should never have displeased you, and then, blessed Lord, you would have had my virginity without end. (1:22, 86)

Christ's response then had been reassuring: 'Because you are a maiden in your soul, I shall take you by the one hand in heaven, and my mother by the other, and so you shall dance in heaven with other holy maidens and virgins, for I may call you . . . my own beloved darling' (1:22, 88). Margery's mystical marriage reflects and seals Christ's earlier promise to her.

Was Margery's mystical marriage her initiation into the unitive way? This question is virtually impossible to answer. It is one thing to include a description of the unitive way in a book of spiritual guidance; it is quite another to sit in judgement upon an individual's spiritual life. 'Experts' in mysticism have generally thought that Margery never reached the heights of mystical contemplation, i.e., the unitive way.[12] Of course, such judgement depends upon what one means by 'the heights'. If, as has been frequent, one equates the unitive way with apophatic mysticism, then one might well conclude this was foreign to Margery. There is no evidence that she was familiar with *The Cloud*, and apophaticism is certainly not her characteristic way to God. On the other hand, if one considers Rolle's heat, sweetness and song as indicative of the unitive way, one's assessment of Margery would be different. After her mystical marriage she reports similar experiences, particularly 'a flame of fire of love' which lasted for sixteen years (1:35, 124–5).

Without prescribing a particular type of religious experience as indicative of the unitive way, it can be said with certainty that over the years Margery grew in union with God. While she never seems to have left behind completely the image-filled meditations on Christ's humanity that gave her such consolation, her prayer does become more quiet and peaceful toward the end of her life, something like the prayer of quiet recommended by Hilton at the end of *The Scale*. As Margery herself says,

> Our Lord, of his mercy, drew her affection into his Godhead, and that was more fervent in love and desire and more subtle in understanding, than was the manhood. And nevertheless, the fire of love increased in her, and her understanding was more enlightened and her devotion more fervent than it was before . . . It was more subtle and more soft, and easier for her spirit to bear. (1:85, 250)

More significant is Margery's constant awareness of the presence of God: 'Her mind and her thoughts were so joined to God that she never forgot him, but had him in mind continually and beheld him in all creatures' (1:72, 212).

In the early pages of her *Book* Margery is self-centred. Even after her conversion, she seems obsessed with her own spiritual development and need for salvation. But the tone of the end of her *Book* is quite different, where she is constantly concerned with the welfare of others. When she is in Rome her confessor advises her to serve a poor old woman, which Margery does for six weeks:

> She served her as she would have done our Lady. And she had no bed to lie in, nor any bedclothes to be covered with except her own mantle. Then she was full of vermin and suffered a lot of pain as a result. She also fetched home water and sticks on her neck for the poor woman, and begged for both meat and wine for her; and when the poor woman's wine was sour, this creature herself drank that sour wine, and gave the poor woman good wine that she had bought for her own self. (1:34, 122)

Similarly, Margery served her husband at the end of his life:

> She took her husband home with her and looked after him for years afterwards, as long as he lived. She had very much trouble with him, for in his last days he turned childish and lacked reason, so that he could not go to a stool to relieve himself, or else he would not, but like a child discharged his excrement into his linen clothes ... And therefore her labour was all the greater, in washing and wringing, and so were her expenses for keeping a fire going ... [She] served him and helped him, she thought, as she would have done Christ himself. (1:76, 221)

The details of these accounts give them authenticity, revealing a patient and generous spirit in Margery. The menial tasks which she had imaginatively performed for Mary and Christ in her meditations become actualized in her care for the needy.

She must have acquired a certain reputation for compassion, for she is frequently called upon to attend the suffering. Particularly poignant are incidents where Margery is able to bring solace to women in situations similar to her own: she comforts a woman tormented by sexual temptations (1:74, 217) and has a calming influence on a woman suffering from a post-partum psychosis (1:75, 217–19). Besides visiting and attending to them, she prays for them until God gives them relief.

Whatever her prayer methods or experiences may have been, Margery's union with God becomes revealed in her acts of charity for others. While she serves them as if she is serving Christ or Mary, it would be equally accurate to interpret her actions as Christ acting in her and through her. Hilton's insight that one's prayer to Jesus eventually results in one's reformation to the likeness of Christ, seems to have been realized 'whole and constant' within Margery. Consistent with the example of Christ and the entire Christian mystical tradition, Margery's contemplative life issues out into service of others.

MARGERY'S GIFT OF TEARS

The most distinctive aspect of Margery's spiritual life is her 'gift of tears'. On practically every page of her *Book*, she weeps, cries, howls, shrieks, screams out her grief – over her own sins, her longing for heaven, her compassion for Christ's suffering, or, increasingly as she grows older, over the sins of the world and sinners' need for salvation. While Margery's behaviour is more boisterous and melodramatic than that of most others, the gift of tears and the doctrine of compunction which they express were staples of medieval piety.[13]

Rooted in Scripture, the patristic writers and the early monastic rules, the doctrine of compunction was promulgated by Gregory the Great, whose writings were present in every medieval library, and whose ideas were quoted in innumerable medieval texts. John Cassian is credited with outlining the four causes of compunction which became conventional in the Middle Ages: 'the pricks of sin smiting the heart, the contemplation of eternal goods along with the desire for future glory, the fear of hell and the recollection of terrible judgment, and the hardness of the sins of others.'[14] The compunction of heart felt inwardly was appropriately expressed externally in the gift of tears. Compunction was seen as a grace, a gift from God, as were the tears accompanying it. They were not something one could produce through effort, but something uncontrollable, given or taken away according to God's pleasure.

The tradition of affective piety begun by Anselm and promulgated by Bernard, Francis, and their followers, added another element to the experience of compunction. Besides grief over sin and longing for heaven, compunction began to include heartfelt compassion for the sufferings of Christ. The paradigm for such compassion was the sorrowful mother weeping at the foot of the cross, represented in expressions of piety like the hymn *Stabat Mater* and in the *pietàs* and other graphic artwork that decorated countless churches. Similarly, Mary Magdalen, already a model for compunction,[15] became exemplary for her grief over the suffering of Jesus. The desire to suffer with these women was encouraged as an appropriate expression of devotion.

The continental women visionaries of the thirteenth and fourteenth centuries cultivated this aspect of compunction to a high degree. The tears accompanying their compassion for Christ's suffering become in them not quiet weeping but uncontrollable loud crying and sobbing, sometimes accompanied by the thrashing about of their bodies in paroxysms of grief. Several of these women present interesting parallels to Margery: Marie d'Oignies (1177–1213), Elizabeth of Hungary (1207–31), Angela of Foligno (1248–1309), Birgitta (Brigid) of Sweden (1303–73) and Dorothea of Montau (1347–94). All of them were married women and, with the exception of Marie, mothers of many children, who struggled for the chance to live a life of holiness. All of them expressed their deeply felt compassion for Christ's suffering through extended bouts of crying, weeping and wailing.[16]

It is quite likely that Margery was influenced by the stories of these women. Marie d'Oignies' story actually played a role in the creation of her *Book*. When Margery was enduring vilification by her neighbours because of her loud sobbing in public, the priest who was her amanuensis, influenced by the criticism, contemplated leaving her. Reading Jacques de Vitry's *Life* of Marie, who sobbed and cried uncontrollably at any mention of the passion, helped convince him that Margery's crying might indeed be evidence of holiness, and so he resumed his task (1:62, 191–3). Margery also mentions that 'Bride's book' was read to her (1:17, 75; 1:58, 182), referring to the *Revelations* of St Birgitta of Sweden, whose cult was extremely popular in England. Margery prayed at shrines of Birgitta in Rome, where she spoke with a woman who had been Birgitta's maidservant (1:39, 132) and visited Syon Abbey, the English house of the order founded by Birgitta (2:10, 290).

The changing nature of Margery's tears may be a better way of charting her spiritual journey than attempting to fit her into traditional categories. As we have seen, she receives her first gift of tears at her conversion, 'great sobbings and sighings' of longing for heaven. In the years of penance and temptation that followed, Margery 'had contrition and great compunction, with plentiful tears and much loud and violent sobbing, for her sins and for her unkindness towards her maker' (1:3, 48). So far Margery's tears are completely consistent with the traditional notion of compunction, involving the twin feelings of sorrow for sin and longing for heaven.

The first significant change in Margery's gift of tears occurs in Jerusalem. While the knowledge of her own sinfulness intensifies her grief, she now cries primarily out of compassion for the sufferings of Christ. Her crying changes from quiet weeping to uncontrollable howling and wailing: 'She had such great compassion and such great pain to see our Lord's pain, that she could not keep herself from crying and roaring' (1:28, 104). These fits of crying were unpredictable and uncontrollable; they would occur 'sometimes in church, sometimes in her chamber, sometimes in the fields.' She 'suffered much contempt and reproof' for her outbursts, for 'the crying was so loud and so amazing that it astounded people' (1:28, 104–5). Consequently,

> As soon as she perceived that she was going to cry, she would hold it in as much as she could, so that people would not hear it and get annoyed. For some said it was a wicked spirit tormented her; some said it was an illness; some said she had drunk too much wine; some cursed her; some wished she was in the harbour; some wished she was on the sea in a bottomless boat. (1:28, 105)

Margery would attempt to hold back her wailing as long as she could 'until she turned the colour of lead', but the more she held it in, the louder would be the crying when it finally burst out from her. Many would not believe she had no control over her sobbing, and accused her of being a show-off and charlatan. However, there were others who understood, and who 'loved her and esteemed her' (1:28, 105).

About ten years after they began, Christ took away Margery's loud cries, which caused her to suffer more abuse, for those who had not believed her crying was uncontrollable now called her 'a false and pretending hypocrite' (1:63, 194–5). All of the rebukes Margery suffered because of her erratic behaviour became a way for her to participate in the abuse Christ endured in his passion. Christ comforted her: 'Now you have the true way to heaven. By this way I came to heaven and all my disciples, for now you will know all the better what sorrow and shame I suffered for your love, and you will have the more compassion when you think upon my Passion' (1:63, 195).

Even though the loud wailing subsided, Margery's weeping continued to the end of her life. However, just as Margery's actions became more directed toward the service of others, so her weeping became more other directed as she grew in spiritual maturity. This began even during the period of her loud wailing, and continued afterwards to the end of her life.

> Sometimes she wept for an hour on Good Friday for the sins of the people . . . Sometimes she wept another hour for

the souls in purgatory; another hour for those who were in misfortune, in poverty, or in any distress; another hour for Jews, Saracens, and all false heretics, that God out of his great goodness should set aside their blindness, so that they might through his grace be turned to the faith of Holy Church and be children of salvation. (1:57, 179)

Ironically, many who had formerly abused her for her loud crying 'desired her to be with them and to . . . weep and cry [for them] when they were dying, and so she did' (1:72, 213). Margery is promised by Christ 'that many thousand souls shall die saved through your prayers' (1:78, 226).

The progression of Margery's gift of tears from weeping over her own sins and longing for heaven, through a period of compassion for and sharing in Christ's suffering, to her weeping for the salvation of others, holds within it the essence of her unique vocation. In company with Christ, her tears and life were meant to be redemptive for the suffering and sins of others. This idea is voiced by Christ in a statement recognizing the homely relationship between Margery and himself:

When you strive to please me, then you are a true daughter; when you weep and mourn for my pain and my Passion, then you are a true mother, having compassion on her child; when you weep for other people's sins and adversities, then you are a true sister; and when you sorrow because you are kept so long from the bliss of heaven, then you are a true spouse and wife. (1:14, 67)

Christ tells Margery her vocation is to be 'a mirror' for others: 'I have ordained you to be a mirror amongst them, to have great sorrow, so that they should take example from you to have some little sorrow in their hearts for their sins, so that they might through that be saved' (1:78, 226). Margery's weeping was meant to be a constant reminder that all had reason to weep and mourn. This may be understood in several ways. Elizabeth Petroff suggests that the public weeping of a woman like Margery 'is an inarticulate cry of one needing a voice . . . in a world that would deny that voice.'[17] Clarissa Atkinson suggests that Margery's struggle was a mirror of new opportunities for 'autonomy, power, and freedom through the life of the spirit' for other laywomen like herself traditionally barred from the pursuit of holiness.[18] Ellen Ross sees Margery as both 'representative of God to humanity' and 'representative of humanity to God', with the twin vocation 'to remind the world of the God of mercy and justice, and, even more, to implore God to be merciful to the public, for whom she is God's minister.'[19] In light of the theme of this book, we might well see Margery as an apt mirror for the deep anxiety of that calamitous age that was the fourteenth century, allowing her cries to sum up its suffering and yet find some redemption in union with the suffering Christ, who assures Margery, 'Your tears and your prayers are very sweet and acceptable to me' (1:78, 226).

7. MAKING CONNECTIONS: THE MEDIEVAL MYSTICS TODAY

The desire of all my soul: your name;
   the desire of my soul: the thought of you.
Preferences, tastes, wishes –
   these bubble up, flicker out
   in the moment's unthinking rejoinders;
   but the desire of my soul is for you.

My soul desires you at night;
   my spirit seeks you within me.
Always, everywhere
   the silver thread firm in a maze of color,
   the theme unchanged through weaving variations,
   the desire of my soul is for you.

                                        Author Unknown[1]

Nothing is more perennial in Christian spirituality than the human desire for God, even though it might be expressed differently in various times and places. The poem-prayer above, a meditation on Isaiah 26:8–9,[2] voices this desire clearly and simply. It was composed by a modern author, but sounds a theme present in the writings of all the mystics studied in this volume. Rolle speaks of his desire to spend his life singing about Jesus, his love. *The Cloud* author writes of the naked intent of the human will for God alone. Walter Hilton focuses on the image of God within and the longing to be reformed to the likeness of Jesus, paradigm for human living. Julian duplicates the prayer's sentiment in her own plea: 'God of your goodness, give me yourself, for you are enough for me, and I can ask for nothing which is less which can pay you full worship. And if I ask anything which is less, always I am in want; but only in you do I have everything' (5:184). Margery Kempe endured abuse and overcame incredible odds to satisfy her longing for union with God. The expression of this theme resonates strongly when twenty-first century folk encounter the medieval mystics. Passages from their writings become our own heartfelt prayers and enkindle in us the desire to seek something analogous to the experiences they describe. This is what makes their writings spiritual classics. They have stood the test of time and continue to speak to readers across the ages, reinterpreted in light of contemporary culture. They put us in touch with the core of our religious tradition, offering us the possibility of its challenge and rich transforming power. In the words of David Tracy, these 'expressions of the human spirit so disclose a compelling truth about our lives that we cannot deny them some kind of normative power.'[3]

This is true in spite of the fact that certain elements in their writings no longer resonate with us today. Indeed some values expressed by these authors present real obstacles to our understanding. Studying the writers in their historical context and in light of the traditions available to them, as in the foregoing pages, can alleviate this problem somewhat. It can help us understand those aspects of their writings that no longer fit the contemporary scene, clearing the way for us to make connections with what can still speak to us. What follows here outlines some of the difficulties these writers pose for us, and then considers how we might none the less pray with each of them today.

MODERN DIFFICULTIES WITH THE MEDIEVAL MYSTICS

The most obvious difficulty is the hierarchical worldview the medieval mystics took for granted, and how this translated into the ordering of the religious life. Because of our modern conditioning by democratic societies, rigid distinctions among laity, clerics, monastics and solitaries, with their ascending order of perfection, are questioned. Even in its medieval setting, this ordering of the religious life was not without difficulty for some. As we have seen, Richard Rolle compensated for his lay status by adopting the 'most perfect' form of religious living, and Margery Kempe struggled mightily to carve out for herself a life of holiness in the world. Such a hierarchical religious worldview is strongly challenged by the Second Vatican Council's *Lumen gentium*, especially in its universal call to holiness.[4] Contemporary practice tries to discourage the exaltation of clerical over lay status in the Church, and attempts to develop spiritualities more appropriate than monastic models for lay living in the world.[5] Certainly neither the solitary nor the monastic life is the most popular form of religious living today, which instead tends to focus on a world-centred, active spirituality. Even the contemplative life is informed by this spirit. The most famous American contemplative of recent times, Thomas Merton, is an interesting example of someone who translated the monastic and eremitic lifestyles into ways of being deliberately concerned for social justice in the world.[6]

A second problem is the threefold way of purgation, illumination and union with God. Though there is certainly some truth for Christian living to be found in the various descriptions of this 'way' of spiritual progress, it has also been subject to criticism. Karl Rahner, for example, objects to its neoplatonic overtones, which suppose that the goal of Christian perfection consists in attaining ever greater knowledge of the secrets of God as the fruit of mystical union with God in prayer. 'From an empirical point of view,' he states bluntly, 'the spiritual life of the great majority of Christians does not end up in [such] mysticism.' Besides, the New Testament view of 'the way and goal of the spiritual life' does not 'give explicit expression to such an orientation.'[7] Such ordering of spiritual progress ignores the personal growth and development of the individual with respect to the biological, psychological and societal conditioning that is part of every human life. Certainly humans grow in their graced relationship with God, which then affects the depth and intensity with which they perform all human acts, whether they are overtly 'religious' or not. Rahner questions whether it is possible to create some universal chart of spiritual progress toward holiness that would apply with any validity to all Christians. His own theology encourages 'finding God in daily life', whatever the circumstances of that life may be.[8]

A related issue is the 'otherworldliness' of the English mystics, due to the same neoplatonic foundations criticized by Rahner. The medieval focus upon heaven and the corresponding fear of damnation are not priorities for us. The need to leave 'the world' behind in order to find God is something contemporary spirituality tries to discourage, emphasizing service to others and finding God in the world as integral aspects of holiness. Even though the English mystics on the whole have a moderate approach to asceticism, and even though none of them, except for Margery, seems overly preoccupied with virginity, it is likely they assumed a life of celibacy to be superior to one involving sexual activity. Contemporary spirituality tries to discourage such thinking and to emphasize the integration of body, mind and spirit.

There is also in some of the English mystics, particularly Rolle and *The Cloud* author, the undesirable tendency to focus upon mystical experience as such rather than the God met through that experience.[9] This tendency eventually developed into the split between theology and spirituality, which was discussed briefly in chapter 3 with respect to *The Cloud*. Focus upon interior experience can also lead to privatism, noted above with respect to *The Cloud*, and Rolle is criticized for this as well.[10]

Finally, in some cases the specific content of what the medieval mystics recommend for meditation poses problems for modern use. While meditation on the humanity of Christ is certainly a staple of Christian prayer, the medieval tendency to focus upon all the bloody details of the various wounds Christ suffered in the passion is distasteful to us. Meditation on Jesus' active life of service and ministry is seen as more beneficial. Contemporary Christology tries to relate Jesus' death more integrally to his whole life lived for others and to his resurrection, rather than isolating that death alone as the instrument of human salvation.[11] The extreme focus on sin and sacramental confession is foreign to us. Similarly, the whole topic of 'bridal mysticism' finds little resonance today, although it still has value for some people.[12]

PASSING OVER AND COMING BACK

In spite of these difficulties, all of which have to do with historical particularities, the writings of the English mystics retain a power to inspire and instruct us. Why and how is this true? One of the best expressions of how spiritual classics remain perennially valid comes from John S. Dunne, who suggests reading stories of past human lives in light of a dialectic between universality and history. Because there is something universal about human experience (however diversely that universality may be dressed), it is possible for the reflective person to 'pass over' to a time and place very different from one's own and find some commonality which can enrich one's own time and place:

> The awareness that comes ... with pursuing ... personal issues in your own life enhances greatly your ability to understand lives other than your own. You find yourself able to pass over from the standpoint of your life to those of others, entering into a sympathetic understanding of them, finding resonances between their lives and your own, and coming back once again, enriched, to your own standpoint.[13]

Dunne thinks that this process adds a depth to our experience which is able to link us to the common story of humankind.

One area where such a process is most relevant, the one that is the focus of both Dunne's study and ours, is the human quest for God, motivated by that deep human desire for God I spoke of earlier. Our modern, secularized world, Dunne suggests, is devoid of the explicit spiritual and temporal mediation which typified earlier, more theocentric worldviews. 'Passing over to others makes them mediators between [ourselves] and God', while 'coming back' to ourselves places us 'once again in the modern situation of unmediated existence', but 'enriched' by the 'time and memory of others'. In the process we find 'companionship with God in time', discovering 'the greater dimensions' of humanity, 'those which reach beyond the self and the individual life story'. In doing this, Dunne believes, we discover 'the face underlying all, that of the compassionate God and the compassionate Savior.'[14] The quotation from Underhill with which I began this book emphasizes the particularity of history, helping us appreciate the variety of God's ways with us. By contrast, Dunne wants us to focus on the commonality of the human experience of God's grace in time, noting parallels and making connections between past lives and our own. The combination of these two insights can help us read and pray with the English mystics today.

Barbara Tuchman entitled her history of the fourteenth century *A Distant Mirror*, deliberately pointing to the parallels that exist between that century and our own time. Certainly the twentieth century rivalled the fourteenth as calamitous, having witnessed horrendous wars, savage acts of genocide and terrorism, escalating poverty and disease, and the deconstruction of reliable systems of learning and faith. Reading the English mystics with a consciousness of their historical context can provide examples for us of people who were not demoralized by the similar disintegration of their own society, but who turned to God for courage and inspiration about how to live in the midst of it. They thus serve as mediators, in Dunne's sense, between God and us, who live in a more radically secular culture. At the same time, these men and women were alert to the positive advances of their time, not the least of which was the development of vernacular literature, which they utilized for their benefit and that of others. Thus, the English medieval mystics can function as 'distant mirrors' for us, fellow Christians on the human journey toward God.

Philip Sheldrake points to the literary genre of spiritual classics as an explanation for how they continue to touch us today. They inspire us, not simply by the content of their teaching, but by the evocative and persuasive power of their language. Speaking of Julian, Sheldrake remarks, 'There is an intimacy of language, and almost poetic use of imagery, which invite the reader into the heart of contemplative experience.'[15] The same might be said of all the English mystics without exception. The passion they feel for their subject comes through their masterful English prose, and sounds a corresponding chord within us, motivating us to seek our own opportunities to open ourselves to God's gracious presence. The relevance of these texts across the centuries does not depend, then, on encouraging a rigid imitation of the practices or lifestyles they describe, but on transmitting to us their authors' inner motivation to seek God, which we can adapt to our own life situations. We are challenged and changed by reading such texts.

On the other hand, as we have learned from contemporary masters of hermeneutics like Paul Ricoeur and Hans-Georg Gadamer, every great symbolic work of literature contains within it a surplus of meaning far beyond the original intention of the author.[16] While it is important to know something of the author's circumstances and purpose in creating the work, our appropriation of it is not limited to those. The meaning of the text comes alive for us in the present, changed somewhat by the perceptions and circumstances of its readers.

Sheldrake uses the apt analogy of musical performance to describe what happens when people today read spiritual classics like those of the English mystics.[17] For instance, a pianist playing a Mozart sonata must be attentive to the limits of the score if what she plays is to continue to be recognizable as Mozart. Yet that pianist also brings everything she is to the sonata, interpreting it expressively for a contemporary audience. The pianist is transformed by the music, but the music is also transformed by the pianist. Something more than what Mozart intended happens through her fresh, creative interpretation. Similarly, the English mystics wrote their texts intending that they be 'performed', put into practice by their readers. We, their readers, can be transformed by the evocative power of these texts. But their meaning is also transformed by us as we bring to them our own presuppositions and questions about the life of holiness, pressing them into service for our contemporary prayer and lived relationship with God. In what follows I suggest ways for us to 'perform' the works of the English mystics by providing representative passages from each that might be appropriate for our own prayer and meditation.

PRAYING WITH RICHARD ROLLE

Richard Rolle is probably the most difficult of the English mystics for modern readers to appreciate. Nicholas Watson admires him as a literary artist, but as 'a clear example of a writer whose time has come, but has also – and past all recovery – gone.'[18] Valerie Lagorio disagrees, calling Rolle 'a man and a mystic for all seasons and time'.[19] While admitting that 'there are features of Rolle's spirituality which are inescapably medieval' and thus do not translate well into modern idioms, Rosamund Allen thinks there are aspects of his thought that remain important for us. She cites as examples his rejection of materialism, the joy he found in God, his lay status, and his efforts to be 'a courteous and considerate teacher'.[20]

I myself find that Rolle's works of spiritual guidance, with some minor adaptations to modern life, are still capable of functioning as reliable guides for any Christian aspiring to holiness. This is because Rolle's understanding of spiritual development is firmly grounded in meditation on Scripture and the imitation of Christ, enduring foundations for Christian spirituality in any age. Rolle's love for the Psalms reminds us of the centrality of the divine office, the recitation of which has been a staple of monasticism for centuries, and which is becoming increasingly popular among groups of laity today for both private and communal prayer. Rolle's genuine joy in God and his desire to sing to Jesus, both expressed in his truly lovely melodic rhetoric, make his writings attractive and capable of evoking similar emotions in us. Rolle's persistent caution against the materialistic accumulation of possessions serves as a valid warning against acquisitiveness in our consumer-oriented society. While the solitary life as practised by the medieval hermits and anchorites might have few adherents today, the need for some quiet and solitude amidst the noise and busyness of daily living has perhaps never been more apparent. Thus, Rolle's focus on the importance of solitude for the life of prayer can serve as a reminder to make time in our lives for contemplation. Finally, in an age that encourages the laity to develop their baptismal call to holiness, Rolle is an interesting example from another time of a layperson who pursued that goal. Along with some of the passages from Rolle's writings cited in chapter 2, I offer the following as appropriate for our own prayer and meditation today.

On the book of Psalms:

This portion of scripture is called the book of Christ's hymns. A hymn is 'the praising of God with song.' There are three properties to a hymn: the praising of God, the rejoicing of heart or mind, the affectionate desiring of God's love. Song is the great happiness of thinking of everlasting things and of eternal joy breaking out in the sound of praising. So it is most appropriately termed 'the book of hymns' because it teaches us to love God with a cheerful mood and with rejoicing and tenderness in the soul, praising not only in the heart but with the voice also, and showing the way to those who are inexperienced.

Prologue to *The English Psalter and Commentary*[21]

On love of God and others:

Therefore, whoever you are who undertake to judge others, you should first examine yourself; and judge yourself so that you, having been correctly judged in yourself, can correctly judge others. For because it is necessary that each person who is striving for the heavenly kingdom should be imbued with a charity that is not feigned, I commend it – that is, charity to God and to neighbour – to you as worthy to be had before everything and in everything; for neither will anyone be able to be saved without it, nor will anyone who has it perish. And so you should know that he who does not love God does not know how to love his neighbour; for in loving God one learns to love one's neighbour and in the love of one's neighbour the love of God is nurtured. But if you desire to feel the sweetness of divine love, it is necessary that you set your whole heart to seek Christ. Thus there is a great difference between the love of God and the love of the world. For at first worldly love is sweet in its way, but in the end it is very bitter. But the love of Christ constrains us to be bitter through penitence at the beginning, yet, gradually growing in us, makes us abound with a marvellous joy.

Judica me 19:9–20:11[22]

On finding Jesus:

I went about through Desire of Riches, and I did not find Jesus. I walked through the Abyss of Delights, and I did not find Jesus. I ran through Lust of the Flesh, and I did not find Jesus. I sat with a crowd of revellers, and I did not find Jesus. In all these places, I sought Jesus and did not find him; for by his grace he signified to me that he was not to be found on earth living softly. So I turned aside by another way, and went about through Poverty; and I found Jesus born a pauper into the world, laid in a manger, and wrapped in swaddling bands. I walked through the

Endurance of Bitternesses; and I found Jesus tired from the journey, hungry, thirsty, weakened by cold, made weary by abuses and insults. I was sitting alone, making myself solitary; and I found Jesus fasting in the desert, praying alone on the mountain. I ran through Suffering and Penitence; and I found Jesus bound, scourged, wounded, given gall to drink, nailed to the cross – hanging on the cross – dying on the cross. So Jesus is not found among the rich but with the poor; not in the midst of the sleek but the penitent; not among the lustful and the revellers but the bitter and the weeping; not in the crowd, but in solitude.

Commentary on the Song of Songs 45:5–22[23]

On the single-hearted search for Jesus:

O good Jesus, it is sweet for me to cling to you, for with you I do not fear torments – but without you I do not know where I will be able to find comfort. For me you are grace going before me. For me you are delight leading me on, and for me you are glory receiving me. So what more should I seek, when I have you, who are everything good? Therefore I have you and I seek nothing except you. What is this? I seek only the thing that I have, and I do not seek anything that I do not have! How then will I be satisfied, if what I have is not enough for me, since I want nothing else? Jesus, you see, is enough for me. But so delightful, so sweet is joy, that however much I have received so far, I do not find my desire satisfied. I will be satisfied when his glory is manifested; . . . Indeed, because the divine glory is very tender and very sweet, ineffable and incomprehensible, the lover will always be satisfied, and, being satisfied, will always desire to love.

Commentary on the Song of Songs 73:17–74:8[24]

On detachment:

> For some say, 'We cannot relinquish everything, we are
> weak, we must keep with us the necessities by which we
> live'; and this is allowed. But it is less a matter of not
> being able than of not daring to suffer harsh poverty and
> wretchedness for God. Still, they can by the grace of God
> attain to the summit of the virtues and can lift themselves
> to contemplation of things above, if they abandon worldly
> occupations and business, and rise up indefatigably in
> prayer and meditation, and possess the things they have
> without loving them, and in possessing them relinquish
> them.
>
> *The Mending of Life*, chapter 3[25]

PRAYING WITH THE AUTHOR OF *THE CLOUD OF UNKNOWING*

The Cloud of Unknowing has become a modern favourite, sometimes for assumptions quite foreign to its author. It seems to
provide a simple, practical method of prayer, relatively free of
ecclesial or doctrinal restraint. In an age when church
authority is increasingly held in question, it is easy to see why
such a work might be popular.[26] However, as most commentators on *The Cloud* insist, it needs to be read in the context of
the Christian tradition which gave it birth.[27] This is undoubt-
edly true. None the less, in our post-modern age, with its
tendency to mistrust absolutes of any sort, the apophatic
approach to God, especially its emphasis on the limitations of
human knowledge of the divine, finds increasing resonance.

I find *The Cloud*'s most helpful element for contemporary use
to be its practical instruction about what to do when one feels
drawn from discursive, image-filled meditation to the prayer of
quiet, something that happens inevitably when one engages in
a regimen of prayer faithfully over a period of time. The practice of centring prayer, including the use of a mantra to quiet

one's inner self, so as to become consciously aware of God's presence and receptive of God's inspiration is something many practise regularly today with profit. *The Cloud* author's practical and sensible advice about this way of praying can be beneficial. Besides the passages quoted above in chapter 3, I offer the following as particularly appropriate for contemporary reflection:

On seeking God alone:

Lift up your heart to God with a humble impulse of love; and have himself as your aim, not any of his goods. Take care that you avoid thinking of anything but himself, so that there is nothing for your reason or your will to work on, except himself. Do all that in you lies to forget all the creatures that God ever made, and their works, so that neither your thought nor your desire be directed or extended to any of them, neither in general nor in particular. Let them alone and pay no attention to them.

The Cloud of Unknowing, chapter 3[28]

On keeping time with Jesus:

In the love of Jesus is your help. Love is so powerful that it makes everything ordinary. So love Jesus, and everything that he has is yours. By his Godhead he is the maker and giver of time. By his manhood he is truly the keeper of time. And by his Godhead and manhood together he is the truest judge and accountant of the spending of time. Knit yourself, then, to him by love and by faith. And in virtue of this know you shall be a regular partner with him and with all who are so well fastened to him by love: that is, with our Lady, Saint Mary, who was full of all grace in the keeping of time, and with all the angels of heaven that can never lose time, and with all the saints in heaven and on earth, who by the grace of Jesus keep time in perfect justice because of love.

The Cloud of Unknowing, chapter 4[29]

On Martha and Mary:

In the gospel of Saint Luke it is written that when our Lord
was in the house of Martha, all that time that Martha was
busying herself with the preparation of his food, her sister
Mary sat at his feet. In listening to him, she had no time for
the busy activity of her sister; even though this activity was
very good and holy, for it is the first part of the active life.
Nor was she paying attention to the preciousness of his
blessed body, nor to the sweet voice and words of his
manhood; though this is better and holier, for it is the
second part of the active life and the first of the contemplative life. She was contemplating, with all the love of her
heart, the supreme and sovereign wisdom of his Godhead,
clothed in the dark words of his manhood. She had no
desire to leave off, not for anything that she saw or heard
spoken going on around her. But she sat unmoving, sending
up many a sweet and longing impulse of love, to beat upon
that high cloud of unknowing between her and her God.

The Cloud of Unknowing, chapter 17[30]

On the simple extension of the will to God:

When you come away by yourself, do not be thinking ahead
of time what you are to do next; forsake good thoughts as
well as evil thoughts. And do not pray with words unless
you feel really inclined to do so. And then, if you feel you
should say anything, do not reckon how long or how short
the prayer should be ... Take care that nothing remains
for your mind's activity but the simple extension of your
will, reaching out to God, not dressed up in any particular
thought concerning God as he is in himself, or as revealed
in any of his works; simply that he is as he is. Let him be
just so, I pray you; do not make anything else of him.
Do not seek to penetrate any deeper into him by subtle
reasoning; let faith be your foundation.

A Letter of Private Direction, chapter 1[31]

On being oneself:

Speak when you like and leave off when you like; eat when you like and fast when you like; be in company when you like and by yourself when you like – as long as God and his grace are your directors. Let them fast who so wish, and live solitary, and keep silence. But you, have God as your guide, who leads no one astray. Silence and speaking, fasting and eating, living solitary and in company – all these can beguile us. And if you hear of any [one] who speaks or is silent, of any who eat or fast who live in company or by themselves, then think and say, if you will, that they know how to act as they ought . . . But take care not to do as they do; I mean apishly, just because they do so. For either you are unable to do so, or perhaps their dispositions are not yours. And therefore avoid acting according to other [people's] dispositions; but act according to your own, insofar as you can discover what they are.

The Assessment of Inward Stirrings[32]

PRAYING WITH WALTER HILTON

Hilton's *Scale of Perfection* is not well known today.[33] This is regrettable, since its theological depth and its flexibility with respect to spiritual lifestyles and forms of prayer make it easily adaptable to modern times. The ideal of opening oneself to be reformed to the image of Christ is the essence of Christian spirituality in any age. Because Hilton leaves the specific 'way' to such reforming flexible, one can translate his teaching into one's own circumstances of life. His astute description of the various movements experienced in contemplation, especially at the end of *Scale* 2, is wise advice that those engaged in regular daily prayer might read with much profit.

More than anything else, Hilton's focus on Jesus as the object of meditation and contemplation makes his *Scale* well worth reading. Such a focus is surely a perennial of Christian spirituality, and, as noted above, some of his meditations on Jesus are among the loveliest I have read anywhere in devotional literature. The heartfelt longing for Jesus they express is able to evoke similar desires in modern readers. The way Hilton speaks of how Jesus appears as one advances in holiness shows signs of being drawn from personal experience. First one has a vague desire for Jesus, to be with him, to be like him. Then one begins meditating upon his life and virtues, often with great feeling and joy. But soon, one begins to leave such meditation behind in favour of a quiet being with him, waiting for him, alert to the inspiration that comes from him. Finally one begins to be aware of the fact that Jesus actually lives through one's daily words and actions, in tune with Paul's realization: 'It is no longer I who live, but it is Christ who lives in me' (Galatians 2:20). Hilton's whole project is to describe this gentle, subtle development, this reformation into the likeness of Christ, which is the true aim and goal of every baptized Christian. There are others who have developed this theme, certainly, in Western Christianity, but none have done it better than Walter Hilton. Some of Hilton's most beautiful passages suited for prayer and meditation can be found in chapter 4 above, but I offer the following also as appropriate for performance today.

On discernment of spirits:

Jesus is knitted and fastened to a person's soul by a good will and a great desire for him, to have him alone and to see him in his spiritual glory. The greater this desire, the more firmly is Jesus knitted to the soul; the less the desire, the more loosely is he joined. Then whatever spirit or feeling it is that lessens this desire and wants to draw it down from its natural ascent toward Jesus in order to set it upon itself, this spirit will unknit and undo Jesus from the soul; and therefore it is not from God but from the working of the Enemy. Nonetheless, if a spirit, a feeling or a revelation by an angel increases this desire, knits firmer the knot of love and devotion to Jesus, opens the sight of your soul more clearly to spiritual knowledge, and makes it humbler in itself, this spirit is from God.

The Scale of Perfection 1:12[34]

On distraction in prayer:

When you want to have the intention of your heart held upward to God in prayer, you feel so many vain thoughts of the things you have done or will do, or of other people's actions, with many other such matters hindering and vexing you, that you can feel neither savor nor rest in your prayer nor devotion in what you are saying. And often the more you labor to control your heart, the further it is from you, and sometimes the harder it is from beginning to end, so that you feel that everything you do is merely lost ... I shall tell you how I feel about this question. When you are about to pray, make your intention and your will at the beginning as complete and as pure toward God as you can, briefly in your mind, and then begin and do as you can. And however badly you are hindered from your first resolve, do not be too fearful, or too angry with yourself, or impatient against God for not giving you that savor and spiritual sweetness with devotion ... Instead, see by it your own weakness and bear it easily, holding your prayer in your own sight (simple as it is) with humbleness of heart, also trusting confidently in the mercy of our Lord that he will make it good – more than you know or feel; and if you do so, all shall be well.

The Scale of Perfection 1:33[35]

On the desire for Jesus:

If you should feel great desire in your heart toward Jesus, either by remembrance of this name Jesus, or by the remembrance and saying of any word or prayer, or by anything that you do, and this desire is so great that it puts out as if by force all other thoughts and desires of the

world . . . then you are doing well in your search for Jesus.
And when you feel this desire for . . . Jesus . . . helped and
strengthened by spiritual power, . . . so much that for the
time the point of your thought is set on nothing created, . . .
but only is enclosed, rested, softened, and anointed in
Jesus – then you have found something of Jesus, not yet
himself as he is, but only a shadow of him. For the better
you find him, the more you will desire him . . . Lift up the
desire of your heart to Jesus – even though you are blind
and can see nothing of him – and say that he it is whom
you have lost, him you want to have, and nothing but him:
no other joy, no other bliss, in heaven or on earth, but him.
And although it may happen that you feel him in devotion
or in knowing, or in any other gift, whatever it may be, do
not rest in it as though you had fully found Jesus, but
forget what you have found, and always be longing for
Jesus more and more, to find him better, as if you had
nothing at all . . . However much you know or feel of him
here in this life, he is still above it. And therefore if you
want to find him fully as he is in the bliss of loving, never
cease from spiritual desire as long as you live.

The Scale of Perfection 1:46[36]

On hearing Jesus:

You are asleep to him rather than he to you, for he calls you
quite often with his sweet secret voice, very quietly stirring
your heart to leave all the jangle of vain things in your soul
and give heed only to him, and to hearing him speak . . .
My daughter, hear and see, and bow your ear to me, and
forget the folk of your worldly thoughts and the house of
your carnal and natural affections [Psalm 45:10]. Look,
here you can see how our Lord calls you and all others who
are willing to listen to him. What hinders you, then, so that
you are unable to see or hear him? Truly, there is in your
heart so much din and clamor of vain thoughts and fleshly
desires that you can neither hear nor see him; therefore

put away unrestful din, break the love of sin and vanity, and bring into your heart the love of virtues, and full charity; and then you shall hear your Lord speak to you.

The Scale of Perfection 1:50[37]

On the name of Jesus:

Your name Jesus is oil poured out [Song of Songs 1:2]. Your name is Jesus: that is, Health. Then as long as I feel my soul sore and sick for sin, hurting from the heavy burden of my body, sorry and fearful for the perils and wretchedness of this life, so long, Lord Jesus, your name is oil shut up, not oil poured out for me. But when I feel my soul suddenly touched with the light of grace, healed and soothed from all the filth of sin, comforted in love and light with spiritual strength and unspeakable gladness, then I can say to you with joyful praise and spiritual might, 'Your name Jesus is oil poured out for me; since by the effect of your gracious visiting I well feel the true interpretation of your name, you who are Jesus, Healing; for it is only your gracious presence that heals me from sorrow and from sin.'

The Scale of Perfection 2:41[38]

On praying with Scripture:

Jesus is the well of wisdom, and by a little pouring of his wisdom into a pure soul he makes the soul wise enough to understand all holy scripture: not all at once in a special beholding, yet through that grace the soul receives a new ability and a grace-given disposition to understand it in a special way when it comes to mind. This openness and clarity of perception is made by the spiritual presence of Jesus: for example, the gospel speaks of two disciples going to the village of Emmaus, burning with desire and talking of Jesus. Our Lord Jesus appeared to them in person, like a pilgrim, and taught them the prophecies about himself; and as the gospel says, . . . he opened the clearness of their wit, so that they could understand holy scripture [Luke 24:27]. In just the same way the spiritual presence of Jesus opens the understanding of his lover who burns in desire for him, and by the ministry of angels brings to his mind the words and the insights of holy scripture, unsought and unconsidered, one after another, and readily expounds them, however hard or secret they may be . . . Holy scripture is vital food, and nourishment full of delight. It tastes very sweet when it is well chewed by spiritual understanding, because in it is hidden the spirit of life.

The Scale of Perfection 2:43[39]

PRAYING WITH JULIAN OF NORWICH

Of all the English mystics, Julian is currently the most popular. This was not always the case. Unlike the works of Rolle and Hilton, manuscripts of Julian's text are scarce, perhaps indicating that *Showings* was little known in her own time. Her popularity today can be explained in part by the burgeoning academic effort, influenced by the women's movement, to reclaim the forgotten lives and works of women of the past. For women in today's Church, Julian serves as a model of one who courageously challenged certain aspects of church teaching, out of both loyalty to the Church and fidelity to her own experience of God. For academics like myself, she is a paradigm for women theologians, scarce indeed in the history of theology. Her theological gift to the Church is only beginning to be explicated and appreciated; it is an excellent example of how spirituality gives birth to theology, and how theology consequently informs spirituality.

Having been rediscovered, Julian has become the subject not only of innumerable scholarly books and articles, but also of popular treatments.[40] The simple, heartfelt nature of her words and imagery have made her the most accessible of the English mystics for today's Christians. Julian is popular because of the nature of her text to inspire, to comfort and to galvanize her readers to action. She intended that the insights she recorded in her book, addressed to all her 'even-Christians', be put into practice. Indeed, she explicitly endorses the 'performance theme' mentioned above as the proper way to access her text, writing at the end of *Showings*: 'This book is begun by God's gift and his grace, but it is not yet performed as I see it. For charity, let us all join with God's working in prayer, thanking, trusting, rejoicing' (86:342).[41] Modern readers are responding eagerly to the invitation.

Besides being written for our performance, Julian's text grew out of her own performance of the message of her revelations. She describes for us, as I indicated above, her own personal experience of the essence of the Christian mystery of salvation: the redeeming Word of God coming into the midst of her suffering. This altered her life forever, replacing her fear of the destructive power of sin with absolute trust in the goodness and love of God. Just as this message was well suited to the anxious atmosphere of the fourteenth century, so it is for today. Grounded in autobiography, the concrete story of a life, Julian's teaching possesses a directness that invites our entrance into the reality it describes.[42] The vividness of Julian's imagery also fosters this possibility. For example, her presentation of a compassionate, motherly God provides for many a fresh way to imagine the divine, encouraging the prayer of trust. Many of the most evocative passages from *Showings* are found in chapter 5 above, but in addition, I offer the following for reflection.

On Mary, paradigm of contemplatives:

> I saw her . . . [as] a simple, humble maiden, young in years, grown a little taller than a child, of the stature which she had when she conceived. Also God showed me part of the wisdom and the truth of her soul, and in this I understood the reverent contemplation with which she beheld her God, who is her creator, marvelling with great reverence that he was willing to be born of her who was a simple creature created by him. And this wisdom and truth, this

knowledge of her creator's greatness and of her own created littleness, made her say very meekly to Gabriel: Behold me here, God's handmaiden ... Just as before I had seen her small and simple, now [Christ] showed her high and noble and glorious and more pleasing to him than all creatures. And so he wishes it to be known that all who take delight in him should take delight in her, and in the delight that he has in her and she in him.

Showings, Long Text 4, 25[43]

God's providence:

I saw most truly that [God] never changed his purpose in any kind of thing, nor ever will eternally. For there was nothing unknown to him in his just ordinance before time began, and therefore all things were set in order, before anything was made, as it would endure eternally. And no kind of thing will fail in that respect, for he has made everything totally good. And therefore the blessed Trinity is always wholly pleased with all its works; and God revealed all this most blessedly, as though to say: See, I am God. See, I am in all things. See, I do all things. See, I never remove my hands from my works, nor ever shall without end. See, I guide all things to the end that I ordain them for, before time began, with the same power and wisdom and love with which I made them; how should anything be amiss? ... Then I saw truly that I must agree, with great reverence and joy in God.

Showings, Long Text 11[44]

On the love of Christ:

With a kindly countenance our good Lord looked into his side, and he gazed with joy, and ... there he revealed a fair and delectable place, large enough for all mankind that will be saved and will rest in peace and in love. And with that he brought to mind the dear and precious blood and water which he suffered to be shed for love. And in this sweet sight he showed his blessed heart split in two, and as he rejoiced he showed . . . the endless love which was without beginning and is and always shall be. And with this our good Lord said most joyfully: See how I love you, as if he had said, my darling, behold and see your Lord, your God, who is your Creator and your endless joy; see your own brother, your saviour; my child, behold and see what delight and bliss I have in your salvation, and for my love rejoice with me . . . How could it now be that you would pray to me for anything pleasing to me which I would not very gladly grant to you? For my delight is in your holiness and in your endless joy and bliss in me. This is the understanding, as simply as I can say it, of these blessed words: See how I loved you. Our Lord revealed this to make us glad and [merry].

Showings, Long Text 24[45]

On sin and God's comfort:

I did not see sin, for I believe that it has no kind of substance, no share in being, nor can it be recognized except by the pain caused by it. And it seems to me that this pain is something for a time, for it purges and makes us know ourselves and ask for mercy; for the Passion of our Lord is comfort to us against all this, and that is his blessed will. And because of the tender love which our good Lord has for all who will be saved, he comforts readily and sweetly, meaning this: It is true that sin is the cause of all this pain, but all will be well, and every kind of thing will be well. These words were revealed most tenderly, showing no kind of blame to me or to anyone who will be saved.

Showings, Long Text 28[46]

On God's promise that all will be well:

Our good Lord answered to all the questions and doubts which I could raise, saying most comfortingly: I may make all things well, and I can make all things well, and I shall make all things well, and I will make all things well; and you will see yourself that every kind of thing will be well . . . And in these five words God wishes us to be enclosed in rest and in peace . . . He wants us to know that he takes heed not only of things which are noble and great, but also of those which are little and small . . . And this is what he means when he says: Every kind of thing will be well. For he wants us to know that the smallest thing will not be forgotten. Another understanding is this: that there are many deeds which in our eyes are so evilly done and lead to such great harms that it seems to us impossible that any good result could ever come of them. And we contemplate this and sorrow and mourn for it so that we cannot rest in the blessed contemplation of God as we ought to do. And the cause is this: that the reason which we use is now so blind, so abject and so stupid that we cannot recognize God's exalted, wonderful wisdom, or the power and the goodness of the blessed Trinity. And this is his intention when he says: You will see yourself that every kind of thing will be well, as if he said: Accept it now in faith and trust, and in the very end you will see truly, in fulness of joy.

Showings, Long Text 31–2[47]

On the soul as God's home:

And then our good Lord opened my spiritual eye, and showed me my soul in the midst of my heart. I saw the soul as wide as if it were an endless citadel, . . . a blessed kingdom, . . . a fine city. In the midst of that city sits our Lord Jesus, true God and true man, a handsome person and tall, highest bishop, most awesome king, most honorable lord. And I saw him splendidly clad in honors. He sits erect there in the soul, in peace and rest, and he rules and guards heaven and earth and everything that is ... And the soul is wholly occupied by the blessed divinity, sovereign power, sovereign wisdom and sovereign goodness. The place which Jesus takes in our soul he will nevermore vacate, for in us is his [homeliest home] and his everlasting dwelling.

Showings, Long Text 68[48]

PRAYING WITH MARGERY KEMPE

Margery Kempe has also come into her own in modern times. Once compared unfavourably with Julian, branded as self-centred, hysterical or psychotic, she has undergone a reappraisal in recent decades, benefiting from the same scholarly retrieval that rediscovered Julian. Her story can be read, as I intimated above, as a warning against the kind of rigid structuring of patterns of holiness that typified her day. Modern critics are apt to treat Margery with sympathy for the abuse she endured, but also with admiration for her forceful and feisty personality.

Because of the autobiographical nature of Margery's *Book,* her work possesses the same directness we find in Julian's text. The movement which Hilton described more abstractly – from simple curiosity about and longing for Christ, through emotion-filled meditations on his life and suffering, through a more quiet being with him in prayer, and culminating in a reformation in likeness to him evidenced in a life lived for others – comes alive in Margery's life story with great vividness. Through this movement, the chaos of Margery's life finds resolution in peace, offering hope to those who encounter chaos in their own lives. Morover, Margery's meditations on the life of Christ and Mary, filled with candour, simplicity, and a charming attention to detail, might be read with profit as examples of personal engagement with the Scripture stories, encouraging similar imaginative contemplation. Margery's text

is also valuable because it provides a rare first-hand glimpse
into the religious life of early fifteenth-century England from
the perspective of a laywoman. Besides the passages in chapter
6 above, I present the following as particularly interesting
windows into the life and spirituality of Margery Kempe.

On God's presence:

Then our Lord said in her mind, . . . 'Though I sometimes
withdraw the feeling of grace from you, either in speaking
or in weeping, do not be frightened at this, for I am a
hidden God in you, so you should have no vainglory, and
should recognize that you may not have tears or spiritual
conversing except when God will send them to you, for they
are the free gifts of God, distinct from your merit, and he
may give them to whom he wishes, and do you no wrong.
And therefore take them meekly and thankfully when I
send them, and suffer patiently when I withdraw them,
and seek diligently until you get them, for tears of compunction, devotion and compassion are the highest gifts,
and the most secure, that I give on earth. And what more
should I do for you, unless I were to take your soul out of
your body and put it in heaven, and that I will not do yet.
Nevertheless, wheresoever God is, heaven is; and God is in
your soul . . . For when you go to church, I go with you;
when you sit at your meal, I sit with you; when you go to
bed, I go with you; and when you go out of town, I go with
you.'

The Book of Margery Kempe 1:14[49]

On visiting Julian:

And then she was commanded by our Lord to go to an
anchoress in the same city who was called Dame Julian.
And so she did, and told her about the grace, that God had
put into her soul, . . . and also many wonderful revelations,
which she described to the anchoress to find out if there

were any deception in them, for the anchoress was expert in such things and could give good advice. The anchoress, hearing the marvellous goodness of our Lord, highly thanked God with all her heart for his visitation, advising this creature to be obedient to the will of our Lord and fulfill with all her might whatever he put into her soul, if it were not against the worship of God and the profit of her fellow Christians. For if it were, then it were not the influence of a good spirit, but rather of an evil spirit. 'The Holy Ghost never urges a thing against charity, and if he did, he would be contrary to his own self, for he is all charity ... Any creature that has these tokens may steadfastly believe that the Holy Ghost dwells in [her] soul. And much more, when God visits a creature with tears of contrition, devotion or compassion, [she] may and ought to believe that the Holy Ghost is in [her] soul ... God and the devil are always at odds, and they shall never dwell together in one place, and the devil has no power in a [person's] soul ... Holy Writ says that the soul of a righteous [person] is the seat of God, and so I trust, sister, that you are. I pray God grant you perseverance.'

The Book of Margery Kempe 1:18[50]

On being thanked by God:

Then our Lord in a way thanked her, because she in contemplation and in meditation had been his mother's handmaid, and helped to look after him in his childhood and so forth, until the time of his death, and said to her, 'Daughter, you shall have as great reward with me in heaven for your good service, and the good deeds that you have done in your mind and meditation, as if you had done those same deeds with your bodily senses outwardly. And also, daughter, when you do any service to yourself and your husband, in meals or in drink or any other thing that is needful for you, for your confessors, or for any others that you receive in my name, you shall have the same reward in heaven as though you did it to my own person or to my blessed mother, and I shall thank you for it.

The Book of Margery Kempe 1:84[51]

On being written in the Book of Life:

One time, as the said creature was kneeling before an altar of the Cross and saying a prayer, her eyelids kept closing together, as though she would have slept. And in the end she couldn't choose; she fell into a little slumber, and at once there appeared truly to her sight an angel, all clothed in white as if he were a little child, bearing a huge book before him. Then this creature said to the child, or else to the angel, 'Ah,' she said, 'this is the Book of Life.' And she saw in the book the Trinity, and all in gold. Then she said to the child, 'Where is my name?' The child answered and said, 'Here is your name, written at the Trinity's foot,' and with that he was gone, she didn't know where. And soon afterwards, our Lord Jesus Christ spoke to her and said, 'Daughter, see that you are now true and steadfast, and have a good faith, for your name is written in heaven in the Book of Life, and this was an angel who gave you comfort. And therefore, daughter, you must be very merry.'

The Book of Margery Kempe 1:85[52]

On fear:

The said creature and her companions entered their ship [for Germany] on the Thursday in Passion Week, and God sent them fair wind and weather that day and on the Friday. But on the Saturday, and Palm Sunday also, our Lord – turning his hand as he liked, trying their faith and their patience – sent them on those two nights such storms and tempests that they all thought they would perish . . . The said creature . . . cried to our Lord for mercy and for the preserving of her and all her company . . . Our merciful Lord, speaking in her mind, blamed her for her fear, saying, 'Why do you fear? Why are you so afraid? I am as mighty here on the sea as on the land. Why will you mistrust me? All that I have promised you I shall truly fulfill, and I shall never deceive you. Suffer patiently for a while, and trust in my mercy. Do not waver in your faith, for without faith you may not please me. If you would truly trust me and doubt nothing, you may have great comfort within yourself, and might comfort all your companions, whereas you are all now in great fear and grief.' With such manner of converse, and much more high and holy than I could ever write, our Lord comforted his creature, blessed may he be.

The Book of Margery Kempe 2:3[53]

On the gift of tears:

A young man who watched her face and manner, moved by the Holy Ghost, went to her when he properly could, alone by himself, with a fervent desire to have some understanding of what might be the cause of her weeping ... She, benignly and meekly, with gladness of spirit, as she thought proper, commended him in his intention, and partly revealed to him that the cause of her weeping and sobbing was her great unkindness towards her maker, through which she had many times offended against his goodness. And also the great abomination that she had of her sins caused her to sob and weep. The great, excellent charity of her Redeemer too, by which through the virtue of his suffering of the Passion and his shedding of his precious blood, she was redeemed from everlasting pain, trusting to be an heir of joy and bliss, moved her to sob and weep, and this was no cause for surprise. She spoke many good words of spiritual comfort to him, through which he was stirred to great virtue.

The Book of Margery Kempe 2:10[54]

NOTES

Chapter 1: The Historical Framework

1. Evelyn Underhill, *The Mystics of the Church* (New York: Schocken Books, 1971), 15–17.

2. For the history of the study of Western spirituality, see Philip Sheldrake, *Spirituality and History: Questions of Interpretation and Method* (New York: Crossroad, 1992), 36–47. For the undesirable separation of spirituality from theology see *idem, Spirituality and Theology: Christian Living and the Doctrine of God* (Maryknoll: Orbis, 1998) and Mark A. Macintosh, *Mystical Theology* (Oxford: Blackwell, 1998).

3. Karl Rahner, 'Reflections on the Experience of Grace', *Theological Investigations* 3 (New York: Crossroad, 1982), 86–90.

4. See Bernard McGinn's splendid history of mysticism, *The Presence of God: A History of Western Christian Mysticism*, which to date has been published in three volumes. For his definition of mysticism see *The Foundations of Mysticism*, xiii-xx, *The Growth of Mysticism*, ix-xi, and *The Flowering of Mysticism*, 24–7 (New York: Crossroad, 1991, 1994, 1998 respectively).

5. Karl Rahner, 'Mystical Experience and Mystical Theology', *Theological Investigations* 17 (New York: Crossroad, 1981), 90–9.

6. For the Victorines, see McGinn, *The Growth of Mysticism*, 363–418.

7. For the Benedictine and Cistercian traditions, see the volumes in this series: Columba Stewart, *Prayer and Community: The Benedictine Tradition* and Esther De Waal, *The Way of Simplicity: The Cistercian Tradition* (London: Darton, Longman & Todd/Maryknoll: Orbis, 1998). For the Cistercians, see McGinn, *The Growth of Mysticism*, 149–323, and, for a representative selection of Bernard's writings, see Bernard of Clairvaux, *Selected Works*, translated by G.R. Evans (New York: Paulist, 1987).

8. There are exceptions to this claim. For example, Douglas Gray thinks it impossible to overestimate Franciscan influence on the development of the English religious lyrics: *Themes and Images in the Medieval English Religious Lyric* (London: Routledge & Kegan Paul, 1972), 21–4. Of the English mystics, Rolle is most affected by Franciscan

influence. For Franciscan spirituality see the volume in this series, William J. Short, *Poverty and Joy: The Franciscan Tradition* (London: Darton, Longman & Todd/Maryknoll: Orbis, 1999).

9. For Dominican spirituality see the volume in this series: Richard Woods, *Mysticism and Prophecy: The Dominican Tradition* (London: Darton, Longman & Todd/Maryknoll: Orbis, 1998), which briefly mentions similarities between the writings of Eckhart and *The Cloud of Unknowing* (120–1). However, efforts to trace some direct influence of the famous German Dominican mystics Meister Eckhart, John Tauler and Henry Suso on the English tradition have been largely unsuccessful. Any similarities between them are probably due to acquaintance with Pseudo-Dionysian thought, probably by way of Victorine interpretation. See the conclusion of Wolfgang Riehle, who explored the possibility of such influence, in *The Middle English Mystics* (London: Routledge & Kegan Paul, 1981), 166.

10. For an introduction to medieval women visionaries and an anthology of writings by and about them, see *Medieval Women's Visionary Literature,* edited by Elizabeth Alvilda Petroff (New York/Oxford: Oxford University, 1986).

11. See Jean Leclercq, *The Love of Learning and the Desire for God,* translated by Catharine Misrahi (New York: Fordham, 1974), 19–22, 87–94.

12. *The Works of Aelred of Rievaulx*, Volume 1, translated by Mary Paul MacPherson OCSO (Spencer, MA: Cistercian Publications, 1971), 83–4.

13. *ibid.,* 84.

14. For a good summary of this tradition, see Clarissa W. Atkinson, *Mystic and Pilgrim: The Book and the World of Margery Kempe* (Ithaca: Cornell, 1983), 129–52.

15. 'Prayer to Christ' in *The Prayers and Meditations of St. Anselm*, translated by Benedicta Ward (Harmondsworth: Penguin, 1973), 95.

16. For this development, together with the more general shift from epic to romance which it exemplifies, see Richard Southern, *The Making of the Middle Ages* (New Haven: Yale, 1963), 237–8. For a brief, lucid article outlining the influence of Anselm, Bernard and Aelred on English spirituality, see Thomas H. Bestul, 'Antecedents: The Anselmian and Cistercian Contributions' in William F. Pollard and Robert Boenig, *Mysticism and Spirituality in Medieval England* (Cambridge: D.S. Brewer, 1997), 1–20.

17. This lyric echoes the famous Latin hymn *Jesu dulcis memoria*, sung for the office of the feast of the Holy Name of Jesus. It was written about 1200 and long ascribed to Bernard of Clairvaux, which has been disproved. However, it might well have Cistercian origins, possibly English ones. It is an excellent example of the style of affective piety described here. See the entry *'Jesu, Dulcis Memoria'* in *The New Catholic Encyclopedia,* Vol. 7 (New York: McGraw-Hill, 1967), 892.

18. 'Jesus, how sweet is the love of thee, no other thing may be as sweet; nothing that people may hear or see is sweet at all compared to

thee . . . Jesus, your love for us was so free that it brought you from heaven; for love you bought me, for love you hung on the tree of the cross . . . Jesus, for love you endured so much woe that bloody streams ran from you; your white sides became blue and blue-black – our sins caused this, alas! Jesus, for love you remained on the cross, for love you gave your heart's blood; love made you my soul's food, your love bought us all good . . . Jesus my God, Jesus my king, You ask of me no other thing, but true love and the yearning of my heart, and love-tears with sweet mourning.' This lyric is listed as no. 89 in the collection by Carleton Brown, *Religious Lyrics of the Fourteenth Century,* revised by G.V. Smithers (Oxford: Clarendon, 1952). It is reprinted with commentary in Gray, *Themes and Images in the Medieval English Religious Lyric*, 122–3. Gray's work is a wonderful introduction not only to the English lyrics, but to the tradition of affective piety in general.

19. *Anchoritic Spirituality: The Ancrene Wisse and Associated Works,* translated and introduced by Anne Savage and Nicholas Watson (New York: Paulist, 1991), 3. For a detailed historical study of English eremiticism, see the classic work by Rotha Mary Clay, *The Hermits and Anchorites of England* (London: Methuen, 1914/Detroit: Singing Tree Press, 1968), and the more recent work by Ann K. Warren, *Anchorites and Their Patrons in Medieval England* (Berkeley: University of California, 1985).

20. For this issue, especially as it affected Richard Rolle, see Nicholas Watson, *Richard Rolle and the Invention of Authority* (Cambridge: Cambridge University, 1991), 7–18.

21. MacPherson, 96–7.

22. Modern English translations of and introductions to all these texts are in Savage and Watson. Recent research suggests all of them were written between 1200 and 1230 by one or more Augustinian canons for one or more groups of women living the anchoritic life. This thesis, developed by E.J. Dobson, is summarized in *ibid.*, 9–15.

23. *Ancrene Wisse* 3 (Savage and Watson, 98).

24. For example, see John Bugge, *Virginitas: An Essay in the History of a Medieval Ideal* (The Hague: Martinus Nijhoff, 1975), 84–110.

25. Atkinson, 185; see also 182–96.

26. Bernard of Clairvaux, *On the Song of Songs,* 2 volumes, translated by Kilian Walsh (Kalamazoo: Cistercian Publications, 1976, 1983).

27. Savage and Watson, 250.

28. *ibid.,* 26–7.

29. For an intriguing commentary on theological possibilities, see Nicholas Watson, 'Visions of Inclusion: Universal Salvation and Vernacular Theology in Pre-Reformation England', *Journal of Medieval and Early Modern Studies* 27:2 (1997), 145–87, especially 166–73.

30. Bernard McGinn (ed.), *Meister Eckhart and the Beguine Mystics* (New

York: Continuum, 1994), 1–14, and *The Flowering of Mysticism*, 18–25.

31. 'Women in No Man's Land: English Recluses and the Development of Vernacular Literature in the Twelfth and Thirteenth Centuries' in Carol M. Meale (ed.), *Women and Literature in Britain, 1150–1500* (Cambridge: Cambridge University, 1993), 86–103.

32. *ibid.*, 99.

33. Robert Lerner, *The Age of Adversity: The Fourteenth Century* (Ithaca: Cornell, 1968); Barbara Tuchman, *A Distant Mirror: The Calamitous Fourteenth Century* (New York: Alfred A. Knopf, 1978).

34. Tuchman, xiii. For English history, see May McKisack, *The Fourteenth Century: 1307–1399* (Oxford: Clarendon, 1959). Much of the following information is drawn from this source.

35. Quoted in Tuchman, 104.

36. C-Text, Passus V, lines 114–15, translated by George Economou (Philadelphia: University of Pennsylvania, 1996), 46.

37. For this fear among the laity along with an alternative view, see Watson, 'Visions of Inclusion', 148–53.

38. See Thomas Tentler, *Sin and Confession on the Eve of the Reformation* (Princeton: Princeton University, 1977) and Mary Flowers Braswell, *The Medieval Sinner: Characterization and Confession in the Literature of the English Middle Ages* (East Brunswick/London/Toronto: Associated University Presses, 1983).

39. For a summary of this literature, see William A. Pantin, *The English Church in the Fourteenth Century* (Cambridge: Cambridge University, 1955), 189–243.

40. C-Text, Passus XI, lines 54–67 (Economou, 100–1).

41. Quoted in Walter Ullman, *The Origins of the Great Schism* (Hamden, CT: Archon, 1948, 1967), 67–8.

42. For a short history see Malcolm Lambert, *Medieval Heresy: Popular Movements from the Gregorian Reform to the Reformation*, Second Edition (Oxford: Blackwell, 1992).

43. *ibid.*, 225–83.

44. *ibid.*, 225.

45. Nicholas Watson, 'Censorship and Cultural Change in Late-Medieval England: Vernacular Theology, the Oxford Translation Debate, and Arundel's Constitutions of 1409', *Speculum* 70 (1995), 822–64.

46. Robert E. Lerner, *The Heresy of the Free Spirit in the Later Middle Ages* (Berkeley: University of California, 1972); Lambert, *Medieval Heresy*, 181–8. For Hilton, see J.P.H. Clark, 'Walter Hilton and "Liberty of Spirit"', *Downside Review* 96 (1978), 61–78. For Julian, see Joan M. Nuth, *Wisdom's Daughter: The Theology of Julian of Norwich* (New York: Crossroad, 1991), 16–22.

47. Lerner, *Free Spirit*, 61.

Chapter 2: The Poet: Richard Rolle

1. Richard Rolle, *The Fire of Love*, translated and introduced by Clifton Wolters (Harmondsworth: Penguin, 1972), 189–92.
2. See for example, David Knowles, *The English Mystical Tradition* (New York: Harper, 1961), 53–66. By contrast, see the positive assessment of Rolle's mysticism in William F. Pollard, 'Richard Rolle and the "Eye of the Heart"' in William F. Pollard and Robert Boenig, *Mysticism and Spirituality in Medieval England* (Cambridge: D.S. Brewer, 1997), 85–105.
3. Nicholas Watson, *Richard Rolle and the Invention of Authority* (Cambridge: Cambridge University, 1991), 258. Watson's analysis of Rolle informs much of what follows here.
4. *ibid.,* 266–8.
5. *ibid.,* 1–27.
6. See Richard Rolle, *The English Writings*, translated and edited by Rosamund S. Allen (New York: Paulist, 1988), 9–21. For an English translation of the lessons from the *Officium*, see Frances M. Comper, *The Life and Lyrics of Richard Rolle* (London: J.M. Dent & Sons, 1928), 301–14.
7. Comper, 301–2.
8. This was a common and acceptable custom in fourteenth-century England. See Ann K. Warren, *Anchorites and Their Patrons in Medieval England* (Berkeley: University of California, 1985), 127–279.
9. *The Fire of Love*, chapter 15 (Wolters, 92).
10. The *Glossa ordinaria* was the standard medieval commentary on the Bible, drawn chiefly from patristic writings and arranged in the form of marginal or interlinear *glosses* (or comments) on each passage of Scripture. It was compiled over an extended period of time by various authors, but by the middle of the twelfth century, it covered the whole Bible.
11. Translation from Watson, *Rolle,* 197–8. Note the prevalent use of alliteration in this quotation, the translation of which preserves the pattern of Rolle's Latin. Alliteration was a favourite figure of speech for Rolle (as for many fourteenth-century poets) and it permeates all his writings.
12. *The Fire of Love,* chapter 15 (Wolters, 93).
13. For a modern translation of a portion of the English Psalter, see Allen, 66–85; for discussion see *ibid.,* 42–3, 65–6 and Watson, *Rolle,* 242–8.
14. Allen, 66–7.
15. Watson, *Rolle,* 240.
16. For the passion meditations and the likelihood of Rolle's authorship, see Allen, 44–5, 90–1, and Watson, *Rolle,* 240–2. Allen's volume contains a translation of the two versions of *Meditation B* (91–124).
17. Allen, 115.
18. See McGinn, *The Flowering of Mysticism* (New York: Crossroad, 1994),

102–4. For the ancient roots of this tradition, see Andrew Louth, *The Origins of the Christian Mystical Tradition* (Oxford: Clarendon, 1981), 54–9, 81–4, 102–3, 163, 171.

19. McGinn, *The Growth of Mysticism* (New York: Crossroad, 1994), 149–57.

20. *ibid.*, 195–7. For the entire treatise plus commentary, see Bernard of Clairvaux, *On Loving God*, translated by Jean Leclercq and Henri Rochais, with *An Analytical Commentary* by Emero Stiegman (Kalamazoo: Cistercian Publications, 1995).

21. See McGinn, *The Growth of Mysticism*: for the Victorines 363–5; for Richard 398–9.

22. *ibid.*, 413–18.

23. *The Fire of Love,* chapter 15 (Wolters, 91–2).

24. *Commentary on Revelation* (Watson, *Rolle,* 67–8).

25. *The Fire of Love*, chapter 15 (Wolters, 93).

26. See Karl Rahner, 'The "Spiritual Senses" according to Origen' and 'The Doctrine of the "Spiritual Senses" in the Middle Ages', *Theological Investigations* 16 (New York: Crossroad, 1983), 81–103 and 104–34 respectively.

27. Watson, *Rolle,* 66. See his discussion of the meaning of each of these for Rolle, 67–72.

28. *The Fire of Love,* chapter 19 (Wolters, 107), my emphasis.

29. The title is from the Song of Songs 5:2: *Ego dormio et cor meum vigilat* ('I sleep but my heart is awake'). The passages which follow are from Allen, 133–42. The page number for each quotation is inserted in parentheses in the text.

30. For this idea see Watson, *Rolle,* 19–20.

31. *The Form of Living*, chapter 10 (Allen, 175); compare with Bernard's *On Loving God*, chapter 10 (Leclercq and Rochais, 30).

32. *Ego Dormio* (Allen, 133–4). Rolle owes his understanding of the nine choirs of angels to Pseudo-Dionysius' *Celestial Hierarchies.* However, his reading the orders of angels as analogous to the ordering of human spiritual development comes to him from Richard of St Victor and Thomas Gallus. See Andrew Louth, 'The Influence of Denys the Areopagite on Eastern and Western Spirituality in the Fourteenth Century', *Sobornost* n.s. 4:2 (1982), 185–200, especially 190–2.

33. *Commentary on the Song of Songs* (Watson, 152).

34. See, for example, *The Commandment* (Allen, 144–5), *The Form of Living,* chapter 8 (Allen, 170–3) and the discussion in Allen, 38–40.

35. *The Mending of Life,* chapter 11 (Watson, *Rolle,* 217).

36. Watson, *Rolle,* 12. This idea is found in a work well known to Rolle: Hugh of Strasbourg's *Compendium theologicae veritatis* 7: 29–30.

37. Watson, *Rolle,* 13.

38. *The Melody of Love,* chapter 1 (Watson, *Rolle,* 175–6).

39. *ibid.*, chapter 48 (Watson, *Rolle,* 183–4).

40. See Hope Emily Allen, *Writings Ascribed to Richard Rolle, Hermit of*

Hampole, and Materials for His Biography (New York: D.C. Heath, 1927), 518–20. For a translation of *Emendatio vitae,* see the version by M.L. Del Mastro (Garden City: Doubleday, 1981).

41. Rooted in the scriptural story of Jacob's ladder (Gen. 28:10–17), the ladder image was commonly used to describe the steps of spiritual progress throughout the medieval period. A famous example is the ladder of humility from chapter 7 of the Benedictine rule. See *The Rule of St. Benedict,* translated by Justin McCann (London: Sheed & Ward, 1970, 1976), 17–22.

42. *The Mending of Life,* chapter 3 (Watson, *Rolle,* 214).

Chapter 3: The Dionysian: The Author of *The Cloud of Unknowing*

1. *The Cloud of Unknowing,* translated and edited by James Walsh (New York: Paulist, 1981), 120–1. References to *The Cloud* will be noted by chapter and page number from this edition in the text; any variations will be enclosed in square brackets. In this quotation, I have changed the author's translation 'a simple reaching out to God' to 'a naked intent to God' which follows the Middle English more closely (120, n. 33).

2. See Harvey Egan, 'Christian Apophatic and Kataphatic Mysticisms', *Theological Studies* 39 (1978), 399–426.

3. For various theories see Walsh, *The Cloud* 2, nn. 3–4; for Walsh's own argument, 3–9.

4. Jan van Engen, 'Preface' to *Carthusian Spirituality: The Writings of Hugh of Balma and Guigo de Ponte,* translated and edited by Dennis D. Martin (New York: Paulist, 1997), xv-xvii. See also Martin's 'Introduction' to the same volume, 3–5 and Walsh, *The Cloud,* 6–7.

5. For Carthusian anonymity, see *ibid.,* xv (van Engen) and 12 (Martin).

6. Phyllis Hodgson (ed.), *The Cloud of Unknowing* (London: Early English Text Society, 1944), 1.

7. Walsh, *The Cloud,* 9–14.

8. Phyllis Hodgson, *Three 14th-Century English Mystics* (London: Longmans, Green & Co., 1967), 22.

9. *ibid.,* 28–30.

10. Medieval translation was not done with the kind of scientific, literal precision that we consider adequate today. Medieval translators felt free to alter their translated works significantly in a variety of ways.

11. Walsh, *The Cloud,* xxv-vi. Modern English translations of all of these works are found in *The Pursuit of Wisdom and Other Works by the Author of The Cloud of Unknowing,* translated and edited by James Walsh (New York: Paulist, 1988).

12. For further information about Denis and his writings see Pseudo-Dionysius, *The Complete Works,* translated by Colin Luibheid (New

York: Paulist, 1987) and Andrew Louth, *Denys the Areopagite* (London: G. Chapman/Wilton, CT: Morehouse-Barlow, 1989).

13. Denis has thus appropriated the neoplatonic *exitus et reditus* theme for his theology: all things have come from God and are destined to return to their source. For a brief discussion of his neoplatonism, see Walsh, *The Pursuit*, 53–4.

14. *The Ecclesiastical Hierarchies* 2:3:2 (Luibheid, 204–5).

15. The work is composed of five short chapters, only seven pages long in the Luibheid volume. 'Apart from the Gospels and some of the Pauline Epistles, there is no single short work in the whole body of Western religious literature that has had so profound a theological influence and so extraordinary a spiritual impact as the anonymous *Mystical Theology*' (Walsh, *The Pursuit*, 51).

16. *Mystical Theology* 1 (Luibheid, 135).

17. Denis's use of this image was probably influenced by Gregory of Nyssa's *The Life of Moses*. See the translation by Abraham J. Malherbe and Everett Ferguson (New York: Paulist, 1978), 91–7.

18. *Mystical Theology* 1:3 (Luibheid, 136–7).

19. *Denis's Hidden Theology*, 'St. Denis's Prayer' (Walsh, *The Pursuit*, 75).

20. *ibid.*, chapter 1 (Walsh, *The Pursuit*, 77).

21. *The Assessment of Inward Stirrings* (Walsh, *The Pursuit*, 140). Cf. *The Cloud* 4:123.

22. Both quotations are cited by Walsh, *The Pursuit*, 153–4, nn. 60–1.

23. Sarracenus's translation was completed in 1167. The English author took quite a few liberties in his translation, expanding it and adding explanations as he deemed necessary. For a comparison of the two, see Walsh, *The Pursuit*, 63–5.

24. *Denis's Hidden Theology*, Prologue (Walsh, *The Pursuit*, 74).

25. Walsh, *The Pursuit*, 66–8.

26. For a brief, lucid account of Denis's mysticism see Denys Turner, *The Darkness of God* (Cambridge: Cambridge University, 1995), 19–49, upon which much of the following is based.

27. For Gallus, see *ibid.*, 186–94.

28. Quoted in *ibid.*, 190.

29. *ibid.*, 191, 194.

30. Walsh, *The Pursuit*, 68. For de Balma's work see Martin, 67–170. In the fourteenth century, this work was attributed to Bonaventure.

31. Walsh, *The Pursuit*, 73.

32. J.P.H. Clark, 'Sources and Theology in *The Cloud of Unknowing*', *Downside Review* 98 (1980), 83–109, 86.

33. Turner, 193–4.

34. For a critique of such undesirable tendencies in *The Cloud*, see Philip Sheldrake, *Spirituality and History: Questions of Interpretation and Method* (New York: Crossroad, 1992), 177–81.

35. *The Cloud* is addressed to a single individual. However, Walsh thinks the bulk of it was probably not written originally for this person, but

was revised with him in mind at a later time. Thus, the work was originally intended for more than one person (*The Cloud*, 9). For the type of readers anticipated by the author see 27:175 and 74–5:262–6.

36. An extended discussion of this topic, using Martha and Mary, the traditional analogues for the active and contemplative lives, follows in 17–23:156–69.

37. *Summa theologiae* 1–2ae, q. 111, a. 2, quoted in Walsh, *The Cloud*, 32. See Walsh's commentary on the doctrine of grace informing *The Cloud*: 26–42.

38. Turner, 99 and n. 40.

Chapter 4: The Master: Walter Hilton

1. Walter Hilton, *The Scale of Perfection*, translated and edited by John P.H. Clark and Rosemary Dorward (New York: Paulist, 1991), 219–20. References to *The Scale* will be made in parentheses in the text, including book, chapter and page number from this version.

2. Phyllis Hodgson, *Three 14th-Century English Mystics* (London: Longmans, Green & Co., 1967), 32, 34.

3. For what follows see Clark and Dorward, 13–18.

4. An inceptor is one who has satisfied all the requirements for the doctorate in a particular profession without actually practising it – probably, in Hilton's case, because of a decision to change careers.

5. Clark and Dorward, 36, 52–3.

6. Jaroslav Pelikan demonstrates the primacy of Augustine in the early medieval period, and, although challenged, reinterpreted and revised, the so-called 'Augustinian synthesis' of theology remained dominant throughout the Middle Ages. See *The Growth of Medieval Theology (600–1300)* (Chicago: University of Chicago, 1978), especially 16–50.

7. 'The area of Augustine's writing is so vast, and his influence so pervasive, that simply to list borrowings from him would be wearisome . . . But perhaps particular emphasis should be laid on his great *De Trinitate*, in which the doctrine of the Trinity is integrated with the whole theological perspective of creation and redemption. Again and again Hilton recalls points found in this book' (Clark and Dorward, 22).

8. For Augustine's theology of image, see John Edward Sullivan, *The Image of God: The Doctrine of St. Augustine and Its Influence* (Dubuque: Priory Press, 1963).

9. Cf. Augustine, *On the Trinity* 7:1:2–4; 15:17:29–31.

10. For the distinction between the mimetic and participatory aspects of image, see Denys Turner, *The Darkness of God* (Cambridge: Cambridge University, 1995), 94–8.

11. For an excellent reflection on the journey within, see *ibid.*, 30–101.

12. The citation is probably a paraphrase of Augustine's famous '*Noverim*

me, noverim te' ('By knowing myself I shall know you') from *Soliloquies* 2:1:1.

13. *Confessions* 1:1:1, translated and introduced by John K. Ryan (Garden City: Doubleday, 1960), 43.

14. For Hilton's sources for these analogies see Clark and Dorward, 174–5, nn. 201–15.

15. In Benedictine monasticism, the experience of compunction, i.e., the feeling of deep sorrow for sin combined with a growing longing for God, was the traditional first step toward contemplation. See Jean Leclercq, *The Love of Learning and the Desire for God,* translated by Catharine Misrahi (New York: Fordham, 1974), 37–41, and the discussion of compunction in chapter 6 below.

16. For Augustine's theology of grace see Roger Haight, *The Experience and Language of Grace* (New York: Paulist, 1979), 32–53, especially 47–8.

17. Cf. Romans 7:15–25; Augustine, *Confessions* 8:5:12, 8:10:22 (Ryan, 180–90, 197–8).

18. For Paul's teaching see Romans 8:2–17 and Galatians 5:16–24. For concupiscence, see Augustine, *De nuptiis* 1:25, 30, 34; Aquinas, *Summa theologiae* 1–2ae, q. 77, a. 5; q. 82, a. 3.

19. Cf. Romans 8:29–30: 'For those whom [God] foreknew he also predestined to be conformed to the image of his Son, in order that he might be the firstborn within a large family. And those whom he predestined he also called; and those whom he called he also justified; and those whom he justified he also glorified' (NRSV).

20. *Mystical Theology* 1.1 (Luibheid, 135), here translated 'brilliant darkness'.

21. For a comparison of Hilton's 'darkness' or 'night' with that of Denis, *The Cloud* and John of the Cross, see Clark and Dorward, 45–9.

22. Hilton follows this list with an explication of each description in detail (2:40, 281–5). For the identification of the 'various men' Hilton refers to, see Clark and Dorward, 322–3, nn. 307–15, 319–27.

23. Cf. Nicholas Watson, *Richard Rolle and the Invention of Authority* (Cambridge: Cambridge University, 1991), 18–19.

24. This meditation probably has its source in Augustine. See Clark and Dorward, 315, n. 200.

Chapter 5: The Theologian: Julian of Norwich

1. Julian of Norwich, *Showings*, translated and edited by Edmund Colledge and James Walsh (New York: Paulist, 1978), 267–8. References to *Showings* will be made in parentheses in the text by chapter (in lower-case Roman numerals for the Short Text, and in Arabic numerals for the Long Text) followed by the page number from this edition. This translation is based upon the Middle English critical

edition also produced by Colledge and Walsh, *A Book of Showings to the Anchoress Julian of Norwich*, 2 Volumes (Toronto: Pontifical Institute of Mediaeval Studies, 1978).

2. For a full exposition of Julian's theology see Joan M. Nuth, *Wisdom's Daughter: The Theology of Julian of Norwich* (New York: Crossroad, 1991). Julian's theology does not follow the scholastic method, but is more like monastic theology (see *ibid.*, 23–9), and probably is best classified as an example of the vernacular theology described by Bernard McGinn (see chapter 1, n. 30 above). For others who have commented on Julian's speculative tendency, see Nuth, 170–1, nn. 9–10, and more recently, Denise Nowakowski Baker, *Julian of Norwich's Showings: From Vision to Book* (Princeton: Princeton University, 1994) and Philip Sheldrake, *Spirituality and Theology, Questions of Interpretation and Method* (New York: Crossroad, 1992), 99–128.

3. Nuth, 31–3.

4. Julian's only such reference is 'Holy Church will be shaken in sorrow and anguish and tribulation in this world as men shake a cloth in the wind' (28:226).

5. See Norman Tanner, *The Church in Late Medieval Norwich, 1370–1532* (Toronto: Pontifical Institute of Mediaeval Studies, 1984), 200, n. 29.

6. *The Book of Margery Kempe*, translated and edited by B.A. Windeatt (Harmondsworth: Penguin, 1985), chapter 18, 77–9.

7. Colledge and Walsh translate this phrase 'to have recollection' of the passion. I prefer 'to have mind' which is in the Middle English, because it remains close to what I think is its scriptural source: 'Let the same mind be in you that was in Christ Jesus' (Phil. 2:5).

8. *Ancrene Wisse* 4 (Savage and Watson, 115–16).

9. See Elizabeth Alvilda Petroff (ed.), *Medieval Women's Visionary Literature* (New York/Oxford: Oxford University, 1986), 9–14, and Caroline Walker Bynum, *Holy Feast and Holy Fast: The Religious Significance of Food to Medieval Women* (Berkeley: University of California, 1987), 120, 199–200, 209.

10. For an introduction to these women together with excerpts from visionary literature by and about them, see Petroff. Some of the more famous are Marie d'Oignies (1177–1213), Mechthild of Magdeburg (1207–82), Gertrude of Helfta (1242–98), Angela of Foligno (1248–1309), Catherine of Siena (1347–80), and Birgitta of Sweden (1302/3–73).

11. While many of these writings circulated in England by the early fifteenth century, evidence of their presence earlier is lacking. See Nuth, 175–6, n. 48. However, since Norwich, through the wool trade, was in direct contact with the low countries and the Rhineland where many of the visionaries lived, Julian could well have heard of them. See Tanner, xvii, 58, 64–6.

12. For a comparison, see Nuth, 12–16.

13. For further discussion see *ibid.*, 175, n. 45.

14. This assumption has been challenged by Nicholas Watson, who thinks the Short Text was written much later than 1373, between 1382 and 1388; consequently the Long Text was completed later also, possibly as late as 1415. See 'The Composition of Julian of Norwich's *Revelation of Love*' (*Speculum* 68: 1993), 637–83.

15. Tanner, 18–42, 191–7.

16. *Ancrene Wisse* 2 (Savage and Watson, 72–3).

17. Robert Lerner, *The Heresy of the Free Spirit in the Later Middle Ages* (Berkeley: University of California, 1972), 47.

18. For the beguines, see the volume in this series: Saskia Murk-Jansen, *Brides in the Desert: The Spirituality of the Beguines* (London: Darton, Longman & Todd/Maryknoll: Orbis, 1998), especially 89–96; Bernard McGinn (ed.), *Meister Eckhart and the Beguine Mystics*; Petroff, 171–8. The beguine movement never took root in England. Interestingly, Norwich is the only city which had communities resembling beguinages; however, since there is no evidence for their existence until 1427, it is unlikely that Julian had ever been a beguine. See Tanner, 64–6; 198–203.

19. Lerner, *Free Spirit*, 195–9.

20. For more discussion see Nuth, 16–22.

21. The extent that Julian's knowledge of Lollardy affected her writing is dependent upon when one dates the writing of the two texts. If the Short Text was written shortly after 1373, the Lollard heresy would not have been a factor; if it was written between 1382 and 1388, as Watson suggests, it could have been on Julian's mind. In any case, Julian probably would have known about the prosecution of Lollard heretics by the time she wrote the Long Text.

22. In Christian theology, the economic Trinity refers to the threefold action of God vis-à-vis the world, revealing a corresponding three-foldness within God known as the immanent Trinity. Julian emphasizes the economic rather than the immanent Trinity in her theology.

23. See John P.H. Clark, 'Predestination in Christ according to Julian of Norwich', *Downside Review* 99 (1982), 79–91.

24. For the origin and development of this idea see Gerhard Ladner, *The Idea of Reform: Its Impact on Christian Thought and Action in the Age of the Fathers* (Cambridge: Harvard, 1959), especially 71–5, 175–7, 184–5.

25. Nuth, 65–72.

26. See Elizabeth A. Johnson, 'Jesus, the Wisdom of God: A Biblical Basis for Non-Androcentric Christology', *Ephemerides Theologicae Louvanienses* 61 (1985): 261–94.

27. Space does not permit here a development of Julian's ecclesiology. For a creative explication of it see Frederick Christian Bauerschmidt,

> *Julian of Norwich and the Mystical Body Politic of Christ* (Notre Dame/London: University of Notre Dame, 1999).

28. Nuth, 74–6.
29. For a good discussion of how Julian's teachings about sin differed from Augustine, see Baker, 83–106.
30. For a complete discussion of Julian's teaching about the possibility of universal salvation see Nuth, 162–8.

Chapter 6: The Pilgrim: Margery Kempe

1. *The Book of Margery Kempe*, translated and edited by B.A. Windeatt (Harmondsworth: Penguin, 1985), 104. All quotations from Margery's *Book* will be cited in the text by book and chapter number with the page number from this edition.
2. Clarissa W. Atkinson, *Mystic and Pilgrim: The Book and the World of Margery Kempe* (Ithaca: Cornell, 1983), 19. See also *The Book of Margery Kempe*, edited by Sanford Brown Meech and Hope Emily Allen, Early English Text Society 212 (London: Oxford University, 1940), xlvi-viii.
3. There are some obvious hagiographical elements in Margery's story, perhaps inserted by her amanuensis in imitation of the *Lives* of holy women. Examples include Margery's 'miraculous' escape from injury when a stone fell on her while she was praying (1:9, 56–7), her ability to see others' sins and predict their status after death (1:12, 61–2), her giving away all her money and depending on God to provide for her (1:37, 128–9), her desire to kiss lepers (1:65, 199; 1:74, 216–17) and her saving St Margaret's Church in Lynn from fire by successfully praying for a snowstorm (1:67, 202–3).
4. For more about medieval autobiography, see Atkinson, 21–8, Elizabeth Alvilda Petroff (ed.), *Medieval Women's Visionary Literature* (New York/Oxford: Oxford University, 1986), 21–8, and Caroline W. Bynum, 'Did the Twelfth Century Discover the Individual?' in her *Jesus as Mother: Studies in the Spirituality of the High Middle Ages* (Berkeley: University of California Press, 1982), 82–109.
5. Atkinson, *Mystic and Pilgrim*, 79.
6. In 1399, a heterodox group of flagellants known as *Albi* or *Bianchi*, whose members dressed in white clothing and 'pretended to great holiness', had been barred from entering England. Margery's dressing in white clothing may have connected her to this group in the minds of her accusers (Windeatt, 318, n. 6). Margery's wearing white clothing was most likely a sign of her chastity, and the fact that she was 'a maiden in her heart'. She may have been influenced here by Marie d'Oignies, who also wore white clothes (Atkinson 33, 50–1).
7. On this point, see Atkinson, 41–8.
8. Windeatt, 326, n. 1.

9. For the notion of liminality, see Victor Turner and Edith Turner, *Image and Pilgrimage in Christian Culture* (New York: Columbia University, 1978), 7.

10. Atkinson, 58.

11. See *Scale* 2:30, 255–6 and the discussion in chapter 4 above.

12. For a history of assessments of Margery, see Atkinson, 195–220.

13. On compunction see Jean Leclercq, *The Love of Learning and the Desire for God,* translated by Catharine Misrahi (New York: Fordham, 1974), 37–41, and Sandra J. McEntire, *The Doctrine of Compunction in Medieval England: Holy Tears* (Lewiston, NY: The Edwin Mellen Press, 1990).

14. McEntire, 45–6.

15. Mary Magdalen, identified with the prostitute who wept over Jesus' feet from Luke 7:36–50 and with the adulterous woman from John 8:1–11, was seen from patristic times as a model for compunction because of her sorrow for sin (*ibid.,* 63).

16. For a discussion of this point, see Atkinson, 157–94 and Petroff, 38–40.

17. Petroff, 39.

18. Atkinson, 220.

19. Ellen M. Ross, *The Grief of God: Images of the Suffering Jesus in Late Medieval England* (New York/Oxford: Oxford University Press, 1997), 122–5.

Chapter 7: Making Connections: The Medieval Mystics Today

1. This poem-prayer, one of a series of meditations for Advent, was given to me almost twenty-five years ago by a spiritual director, and it has been a staple of my daily prayer ever since. I do not know the author.

2. 'In the path of your judgements, O Lord, we wait for you; your name and your renown are the soul's desire. My soul yearns for you in the night, my spirit within me earnestly seeks you' (NRSV). This is the passage that Hilton uses to develop his theme of the 'night' intervening between reform in faith and the beginning of reform in feeling (*Scale* 2:24, 234; see chapter 4 above).

3. David Tracy, *The Analogical Imagination: Christian Theology and the Culture of Pluralism* (New York: Crossroad, 1986), 108; for further discussion of the religious classic, see 99–178.

4. See especially Chapter 5: 'The Universal Call to Holiness' in *Vatican Council II: The Basic Sixteen Documents*, edited by Austin Flannery (Northport, NY: Costello Publishing Company, 1996), 58–65.

5. For example, see Edward C. Sellner, 'Lay Spirituality' in *The New Dictionary of Catholic Spirituality*, edited by Michael Downey (Collegeville: Liturgical Press, 1993), 589–96.

6. See, in particular, his *Contemplation in a World of Action* (Garden

City: Doubleday, 1971) and *Conjectures of a Guilty Bystander* (Garden City: Doubleday, 1966).

7. 'Reflections on the Problem of the Gradual Ascent to Christian Perfection', *Theological Investigations* 3 (New York: Crossroad, 1982), 22.

8. For the Ignatian roots of this idea see Rahner's own 'The Ignatian Mysticism of Joy in the World' in *Theological Investigations* 3 (New York: Crossroad, 1982), 277–93. For brief studies of Rahner in this regard, see James J. Bacik, 'Karl Rahner: Finding God in Daily Life' in his *Contemporary Theologians* (Chicago: Thomas More Press, 1989), 13–25, and William V. Dych, *Karl Rahner* (Collegeville: The Liturgical Press, 1992), especially 4–31.

9. For a history of this development, see Philip Sheldrake, *Spirituality and History: Questions of Interpretation and Method* (New York: Crossroad, 1992), 40–7.

10. Mark A. McIntosh, *Mystical Theology* (Oxford: Blackwell, 1998), 72–5.

11. See, for example, Dermot A. Lane, *The Reality of Jesus: An Essay in Christology* (New York: Paulist, 1975), 39–43.

12. See Janet Ruffing, 'Encountering Love Mysticism: Issues in Supervision', *Presence: An International Journal of Spiritual Direction* 1:1 (1995), 20–33. It is instructive that Ruffing finds it necessary to assist spiritual directors in dealing with this type of experience. It should be noted that generally speaking, with the exception of Rolle and Margery, the English mystics took a much more restrained approach to this form of spirituality than is found in many of their contemporaries.

13. John S. Dunne, *A Search for God in Time and Memory* (Notre Dame: University of Notre Dame, 1967), viii–ix.

14. *ibid.*, xi.

15. Sheldrake, *Spirituality and History*, 164.

16. Paul Ricoeur, *Interpretation Theory: Discourse and the Surplus of Meaning* (Fort Worth: Texas Christian University, 1976); Hans-Georg Gadamer, *Truth and Method* (New York: Crossroad, 1986).

17. *Spirituality and History*, 171–2. The entire seventh chapter of this book (163–87) is a helpful summary of recent hermeneutical theory with respect to classic texts.

18. Nicholas Watson, *Richard Rolle and the Invention of Authority* (Cambridge: Cambridge University, 1991), 269.

19. 'Preface' in Richard Rolle, *The English Writings*, translated and edited by Rosamund S. Allen (New York: Paulist, 1988), 1.

20. *ibid.*, 61–3

21. *ibid.*, 68.

22. Watson, *Rolle*, 83–4.

23. *ibid.*, 149–50.

24. *ibid.*, 152.

25. *ibid.*, 215.
26. For discussion, see Sheldrake, *Spirituality and History,* 177–8.
27. See *The Cloud of Unknowing,* translated and edited by James Walsh (New York: Paulist, 1981), 1–2.
28. *ibid.*, 119–20.
29. *ibid.*, 125.
30. *ibid.*, 156–7.
31. *ibid.*, 219–20.
32. *ibid.*, 143.
33. For example, in their otherwise excellent collection of essays on the English mystics, *Mysticism and Spirituality in Medieval England* (Cambridge: D.S. Brewer, 1997), Pollard and Boenig do not include an essay on Hilton.
34. Walter Hilton, *The Scale of Perfection*, translated and edited by John P.H. Clark and Rosemary Dorward (New York: Paulist, 1991), 86.
35. *ibid.*, 103–4.
36. *ibid.*, 119.
37. *ibid.*, 122–3.
38. *ibid.*, 286.
39. *ibid.*, 293–4.
40. For academic treatments see the notes to chapter 5 above. For some popular treatments see Sheila Upjohn, *Why Julian Now? A Voyage of Discovery* (Grand Rapids: Eerdmans, 1997); *The Wisdom of Julian of Norwich,* compiled and introduced by Monica Furlong (Grand Rapids: Eerdmans, 1996); Carol Luebering, *A Retreat with Job & Julian of Norwich: Trusting That All Will Be Well* (Cincinnati: St Anthony Messenger Press, 1995); Gloria Durka, *Praying with Julian of Norwich* (Winona: Saint Mary's Press, 1989); *Julian,* videorecording of a play by J. Janda, adapted by J. Michael Sparough and Roberta Nobleman (Ramsey: Paulist, 1985).
41. A particularly creative interpretation of the implications of Julian's teachings for ecclesiology is provided by Frederick Christian Bauerschmidt, *Julian of Norwich and the Mystical Body Politic of Christ* (Notre Dame/London: University of Notre Dame, 1999), 191–201.
42. For a study of Julian's theology as autobiography, see Christopher Abbott, *Julian of Norwich: Autobiography and Theology* (Cambridge: D. S. Brewer, 1999).
43. Julian of Norwich, *Showings*, translated and edited by Edmund Colledge and James Walsh (New York: Paulist, 1978), 182, 222–3.
44. *ibid.*, 198–9.
45. *ibid.*, 220–1.
46. *ibid.*, 225.
47. *ibid.*, 229–32.
48. *ibid.*, 312–13.
49. *The Book of Margery Kempe*, translated and edited by B.A. Windeatt (Harmondsworth: Penguin, 1985), 66.

50. *ibid.*, 77–8.
51. *ibid.*, 244.
52. *ibid.*, 247–8.
53. *ibid.*, 273–4.
54. *ibid.*, 290–1.

BIBLIOGRAPHY

Editions of Primary Sources:

Aelred of Rievaulx. *The Works of Aelred of Rievaulx*, volume 1, translated by Mary Paul MacPherson ocso, Spencer, MA, Cistercian Publications, 1971.

Anchoritic Spirituality: The Ancrene Wisse and Associated Works, translated and introduced by Anne Savage and Nicholas Watson, New York, Paulist, 1991.

Anselm of Canterbury. *The Prayers and Meditations of St. Anselm,* translated by Benedicta Ward, Harmondsworth, Penguin, 1973.

Augustine of Hippo. *Confessions,* translated and edited by John K. Ryan, Garden City, Doubleday, 1960.

Benedict of Nursia. *The Rule of St. Benedict,* translated by Justin McCann, London, Sheed & Ward, 1970, 1976.

Bernard of Clairvaux. *On Loving God,* translated by Jean Leclercq and Henri Rochais, Kalamazoo, Cistercian Publications, 1995.

On the Song of Songs, 2 volumes, translated by Kilian Walsh ocso, Kalamazoo, Cistercian Publications, 1976, 1983.

Selected Works, translated by G.R. Evans, New York, Paulist, 1987.

Carthusian Spirituality: The Writings of Hugh of Balma and Guigo de Ponte, translated and edited by Dennis D. Martin, New York, Paulist, 1997.

Cloud of Unknowing, edited by Phyllis Hodgson, London, Early English Text Society, 1944.

Translated and edited by James Walsh, New York, Paulist, 1981.

Gregory of Nyssa. *The Life of Moses,* translated by Abraham J. Malherbe and Everett Ferguson, New York, Paulist, 1978.

Hilton, Walter. *The Scale of Perfection,* translated and edited by John P.H. Clark and Rosemary Dorward, New York, Paulist, 1991.

Julian of Norwich. *A Book of Showings to the Anchoress Julian of Norwich,* 2 volumes, edited by Edmund Colledge and James Walsh, Toronto, Pontifical Institute of Mediaeval Studies, 1978.

Showings, translated and edited by Edmund Colledge and James Walsh, New York, Paulist, 1978.

Kempe, Margery. *The Book of Margery Kempe,* edited by Sanford Brown
   Meech and Hope Emily Allen, London, Oxford University, 1940.
   The Book of Margery Kempe, translated and edited by B.A. Windeatt,
   Harmondsworth, Penguin, 1985.
Langland, William. *Piers Plowman,* C-Text, translated by George Econ-
   omou, Philadelphia, University of Pennsylvania, 1996.
Pseudo-Dionysius. *The Complete Works,* translated by Colin Luibheid,
   New York, Paulist, 1987.
*Pursuit of Wisdom and Other Works by the Author of The Cloud of
   Unknowing,* translated and edited by James Walsh, New York,
   Paulist, 1988.
Religious Lyrics of the Fourteenth Century, edited by Carleton Brown,
   revised by G.V. Smithers, Oxford, Clarendon, 1952.
Rolle, Richard. *The English Writings,* translated and edited by Rosamund
   S. Allen, New York, Paulist, 1988.
   The Fire of Love, translated and introduced by Clifton Wolters, Har-
   mondsworth, Penguin, 1972.
   The Mending of Life, translated by M.L. Del Mastro, Garden City,
   Doubleday, 1981.

Secondary Sources:

Abbott, Christopher. *Julian of Norwich: Autobiography and Theology,*
   Cambridge, D.S. Brewer, 1999.
Allen, Hope Emily. *Writings Ascribed to Richard Rolle, Hermit of Hampole,
   and Materials for His Biography,* New York, D.C. Heath, 1927.
Atkinson, Clarissa W. *Mystic and Pilgrim: The Book and the World of
   Margery Kempe,* Ithaca, Cornell, 1983.
Baker, Denise Nowakowski. *Julian of Norwich's Showings: From Vision to
   Book,* Princeton, Princeton University, 1994.
Bauerschmidt, Frederick Christian. *Julian of Norwich and the Mystical
   Body Politic of Christ,* Notre Dame/London, University of Notre
   Dame, 1999.
Braswell, Mary Flowers. *The Medieval Sinner: Characterization and Con-
   fession in the Literature of the English Middle Ages,* East Brunswick/
   London/Toronto, Associated University Presses, 1983.
Bugge, John. *Virginitas: An Essay in the History of a Medieval Ideal,* The
   Hague, Martinus Nijhoff, 1975.
Bynum, Caroline Walker. *Holy Feast and Holy Fast: the Religious Signifi-
   cance of Food to Medieval Women,* Berkeley, University of California,
   1987.
   Jesus as Mother: Studies in the Spirituality of the High Middle Ages,
   Berkeley, University of California, 1982.
Clark, John P.H. 'Predestination in Christ according to Julian of Norwich',
   Downside Review 99 (1982), 79–91.

'Sources and Theology in *The Cloud of Unknowing*', *Downside Review* 98 (1980), 83–109.

'Walter Hilton and "Liberty of Spirit"', *Downside Review* 96 (1978), 61–78.

Clay, Rotha Mary. *The Hermits and Anchorites of England,* London, Methuen, 1914/Detroit, Singing Tree Press, 1968.

Comper, Frances M. *The Life and Lyrics of Richard Rolle,* London, J.M. Dent & Sons, 1928.

De Waal, Esther. *The Way of Simplicity: The Cistercian Tradition,* London, Darton, Longman & Todd/Maryknoll, Orbis, 1998.

Dunne, John S. *A Search for God in Time and Memory,* Notre Dame, University of Notre Dame, 1967.

Egan, Harvey. 'Christian Apophatic and Kataphatic Mysticisms', *Theological Studies* 39 (1978), 399–426.

Gadamer, Hans-Georg. *Truth and Method,* New York, Crossroad, 1986.

Gray, Douglas. *Themes and Images in the Medieval English Religious Lyric,* London, Routledge & Kegan Paul, 1972.

Haight, Roger. *The Experience and Language of Grace,* New York, Paulist, 1979.

Hodgson, Phyllis. *Three 14th-Century English Mystics,* London, Longmans, Green & Co., 1967.

Johnson, Elizabeth A. 'Jesus, the Wisdom of God: A Biblical Basis for Non-Androcentric Christology', *Ephemerides Theologicae Louvanienses* 61 (1985), 261–94.

Knowles, David. *The English Mystical Tradition,* New York, Harper, 1961.

Ladner, Gerhard. *The Idea of Reform: Its Impact on Christian Thought and Action in the Age of the Fathers,* Cambridge, Harvard, 1959.

Lambert, Malcolm. *Medieval Heresy: Popular Movements from the Gregorian Reform to the Reformation,* second edition, Oxford, Blackwell, 1992.

Lane, Dermot A. *The Reality of Jesus: An Essay in Christology,* New York, Paulist, 1975.

Leclercq, Jean. *The Love of Learning and the Desire for God: A Study of Monastic Culture,* translated by Catharine Misrahi, New York, Fordham, 1974.

Lerner, Robert. *The Age of Adversity: The Fourteenth Century,* Ithaca, Cornell, 1968.

The Heresy of the Free Spirit in the Later Middle Ages, Berkeley, University of California, 1972.

Louth, Andrew. *Denys the Areopagite,* London, G. Chapman/Wilton, CT, Morehouse-Barlow, 1989.

'The Influence of Denys the Areopagite on Eastern and Western Spirituality in the Fourteenth Century', *Sobornost* n.s. 4:2 (1982), 185–200.

The Origins of the Christian Mystical Tradition, Oxford, Clarendon, 1981.

Macintosh, Mark A. *Mystical Theology,* Oxford, Blackwell, 1998.

McEntire, Sandra J. *The Doctrine of Compunction in Medieval England: Holy Tears,* Lewiston, NY, The Edwin Mellen Press, 1990.

McGinn, Bernard. *The Foundations of Mysticism,* New York, Crossroad, 1991.

The Growth of Mysticism, New York, Crossroad, 1994.

The Flowering of Mysticism, New York, Crossroad, 1998.

(ed.). *Meister Eckhart and the Beguine Mystics,* New York, Continuum, 1994.

McKisack, May. *The Fourteenth Century: 1307–1399,* Oxford, Clarendon, 1959.

Merton, Thomas. *Conjectures of a Guilty Bystander,* Garden City, Doubleday, 1966.

Contemplation in a World of Action, Garden City, Doubleday, 1971.

Millet, Bella. 'Women in No Man's Land: English Recluses and the Development of Vernacular Literature in the Twelfth and Thirteenth Centuries', in *Women and Literature in Britain, 1150–1500,* edited by Carol M. Meale, Cambridge, Cambridge University, 1993.

Murk-Jansen, Saskia. *Brides in the Desert: The Spirituality of the Beguines,* London, Darton, Longman & Todd/Maryknoll, Orbis, 1998.

Nuth, Joan M. *Wisdom's Daughter: The Theology of Julian of Norwich,* New York, Crossroad, 1991, 16–22.

Pantin, William A. *The English Church in the Fourteenth Century,* Cambridge, Cambridge University, 1955.

Pelikan, Jaroslav. *The Growth of Medieval Theology (600–1300),* Chicago, University of Chicago, 1978.

Petroff, Elizabeth Alvilda (ed.). *Medieval Women's Visionary Literature,* New York/Oxford, Oxford University, 1986.

Pollard, William F. and Robert Boenig. *Mysticism and Spirituality in Medieval England,* Cambridge, D.S. Brewer, 1997.

Rahner, Karl. 'The Doctrine of the "Spiritual Senses" in the Middle Ages', *Theological Investigations* 16, New York, Crossroad, 1983, 104–34.

'The Ignatian Mysticism of Joy in the World', *Theological Investigations* 3, New York, Crossroad, 1982, 277–93.

'Mystical Experience and Mystical Theology', *Theological Investigations* 17, New York, Crossroad, 1981, 90–9.

'Reflections on the Experience of Grace', *Theological Investigations* 3, New York, Crossroad, 1982, 86–90.

'Reflections on the Problem of the Gradual Ascent to Christian Perfection', *Theological Investigations* 3, New York, Crossroad, 1982, 3–23.

'The "Spiritual Senses" according to Origen', *Theological Investigations* 16, New York, Crossroad, 1983, 81–103.

Ricoeur, Paul. *Interpretation Theory: Discourse and the Surplus of Meaning,* Fort Worth, Texas Christian University Press, 1976.

Riehle, Wolfgang. *The Middle English Mystics,* London, Routledge & Kegan Paul, 1981.

Ross, Ellen M. *The Grief of God: Images of the Suffering Jesus in Late Medieval England,* New York/Oxford, Oxford University Press, 1997.

Ruffing, Janet. 'Encountering Love Mysticism: Issues in Supervision', *Presence: An International Journal of Spiritual Direction* 1:1 (1995), 20–33.

Sellner, Edward C. 'Lay Spirituality', *The New Dictionary of Catholic Spirituality,* edited by Michael Downey, Collegeville, Liturgical Press, 1993, 589–96.

Sheldrake, Philip. *Spirituality and History: Questions of Interpretation and Method,* New York, Crossroad, 1992.

  Spirituality and Theology: Christian Living and the Doctrine of God, Maryknoll, Orbis, 1998.

Short, William J. *Poverty and Joy: The Franciscan Tradition,* London, Darton, Longman & Todd/Maryknoll: Orbis, 1999.

Southern, Richard. *The Making of the Middle Ages,* New Haven, Yale, 1963.

Stewart, Columba. *Prayer and Community: The Benedictine Tradition,* London, Darton, Longman & Todd/Maryknoll, Orbis, 1998.

Sullivan, John Edward. *The Image of God: The Doctrine of St. Augustine and Its Influence,* Dubuque, Priory Press, 1963.

Tanner, Norman. *The Church in Late Medieval Norwich, 1370–1532,* Toronto, Pontifical Institute of Mediaeval Studies, 1984.

Tentler, Thomas. *Sin and Confession on the Eve of the Reformation,* Princeton, Princeton University, 1977.

Tracy, David. *The Analogical Imagination: Christian Theology and the Culture of Pluralism,* New York, Crossroad, 1986.

Tuchman, Barbara. *A Distant Mirror: The Calamitous Fourteenth Century,* New York, Alfred A. Knopf, 1978.

Turner, Denys. *The Darkness of God,* Cambridge, Cambridge University, 1995.

Turner, Victor and Edith Turner. *Image and Pilgrimage in Christian Culture,* New York, Columbia University, 1978.

Warren, Ann K. *Anchorites and Their Patrons in Medieval England,* Berkeley, University of California, 1985.

Watson, Nicholas. 'Censorship and Cultural Change in Late-Medieval England: Vernacular Theology, the Oxford Translation Debate, and Arundel's Constitutions of 1409', *Speculum* 70 (1995), 822–42.

  'The Composition of Julian of Norwich's *Revelation of Love*', *Speculum* 68 (1993), 637–83.

  Richard Rolle and the Invention of Authority, Cambridge, Cambridge University, 1991.

  'Visions of Inclusion: Universal Salvation and Vernacular Theology in Pre-Reformation England', *Journal of Medieval and Early Modern Studies* 27:2 (1997), 145–87.

Woods, Richard. *Mysticism and Prophecy: The Dominican Tradition,* London, Darton, Longman & Todd/Maryknoll: Orbis, 1998.

Ullman, Walter. *The Origins of the Great Schism,* Hamden, CT, Archon, 1948, 1967.

Underhill, Evelyn. *The Mystics of the Church,* New York, Schocken Books, 1971.